PROLEGOMENA
TO THE
PSYCHOLOGICAL
STUDY
OF RELIGION

PROLEGOMENA
TO THE
PSYCHOLOGICAL
STUDY
OF RELIGION

Benjamin Beit-Hallahmi

Lewisburg
Bucknell University Press
London and Toronto: Associated University Presses

Associated University Presses
440 Forsgate Drive
Cranbury, NJ 08512

Associated University Presses
25 Sicilian Avenue
London WC1A 2QH, England

Associated University Presses
P.O. Box 488, Port Credit
Mississauga, Ontario
Canada L5G 4M2

The paper used in this publication meets the requirements of the American National Standard for Permanence of Paper for Printed Library Materials Z39.48-1984.

Library of Congress Cataloging-in-Publication Data

Beit-Hallahmi, Benjamin.
 Prolegomena to the psychological study of religion.

 Bibliography: p.
 Includes index.
 1. Psychology, Religious.   2. Psychology and religion.
I. Title.
BL53.B37   1989   200'.1'9   88-48020
ISBN 0-8387-5159-8 (alk. paper)

Contents

PREFACE

Like every book, this one represents the culmination of many years of work, trials, and errors. In overcoming many errors and accomplishing my work, I have been privileged to enjoy the support of several institutions and many colleagues. I would like to mention the support of the department of psychology at Michigan State University, where in 1978–80 I started formulating some of these ideas, and of the University of Haifa, my academic home for many years. In particular, I would like to mention the Research Authority at the University of Haifa, which has made the preparation of the manuscript possible.

Among my colleagues, who have been most generous and patient with me, I would like to name Peter Homans, Michael Argyle, Lewis R. Rambo, and H. Newton Malony.

This book is a tribute to their encouragement, support, and wisdom. Whatever faults the reader may find in it are the author's charge, to be corrected with more help in the future.

PROLEGOMENA
TO THE
PSYCHOLOGICAL
STUDY
OF RELIGION

1

DEFINING THE FIELD AND THE TASK

Psychology as an intellectual tradition and psychology as a academic discipline (and the two are sometimes far apart) have always made attempts to explain the phenomena of religion, both individual and social. The success of these attempts may be judged on the basis of their congruence with the rest of psychology, or on the basis of their value for scholars in other disciplines studying religion, such as historians and sociologists.

This essay consists of a naturally selective and personal review of contributions to the psychological study of religion, together with a couple of modest attempts to contribute to a better theoretical approach to the field. My methodology is based in as much openness as possible to a variety of sources and viewpoints. In the study of religion, both conventional, academic work and psychodynamic, "soft," insights are pursued and regarded as legitimate. Both should be equally open to criticism, and every research effort should start with a clear definition that limits the objects of study and formulates the system of observation.

A Working Definition of Religion

By the mere act of offering a psychological working definition of religion I am getting a bit ahead of my story, presenting both the products of social science scholarship and a direction for my presentation in the rest of the monograph.

Following Alatas (1977) I will define religion as a sphere of human activity that includes the seven elements listed below:

1. Belief in a supernatural being or beings, and belief that human beings will establish a personal relationship with that being or beings.

2. Certain rites and beliefs, in addition to those in 1., that are sanctioned by supernatural reality.

3. The division of life into the sacred and the profane.

4. Belief that the supernatural world communicates through human messengers.

5. The attempt to order life in harmony with supernatural designs.

6. Belief that revealed truth supercedes other human efforts at understanding the world.

7. The practice of creating a community of believers.

While this list may be too narrow to include some traditions commonly referred to as religions, it is broad enough to cover what to most human beings is connoted by religion, through their concrete historical experience.

The problem of defining religion is not only a scholarly or a theoretical one. It does have many serious secular, legal, and political implications in many contemporary nation-states, where legal status is tied to questions of religious traditions (e.g., Bowser 1977). A psychological definition of religion, as opposed to a legal one, attempts to delineate what is universal in all the concrete experiences and behaviors of humans that are recognized as relating to religion. The working definition of religion used here is the " . . . straightforward, everyday, limited definition of religion as a system of beliefs in divine or superhuman power, and practices of worship or other rituals directed towards such a power" (Argyle and Beit-Hallahmi 1975, 1). This definition, while being conservative for some tastes, has the advantages of being concrete, historical, and close to the direct experience of the proverbial man on the street, the common believer. There is a large gap between religion as it is recognized directly in the culture and the definitions of religion offered by theologians and philosophers. There is a whole language of supposedly religious discourse that is shared by the people who read and write books about theology (very often the same people, I suspect). The psychological definition of religion has to be close to that which real people experience and recognize immediately, and such substantive definitions are in line with the traditions of scholarship in the study of religion.

Durkheim (1915) observed that all religions " . . . presuppose a classification of all things . . . into two classes of opposed groups . . . *profane and sacred,*" (37). From this observation, which has deep psychological significance, Durkheim went on to develop his own definition of religion: "A religion is a unified system of beliefs and practices relative to sacred things, that is to say, things set apart and forbidden—beliefs and practices which unite into one single moral community called a Church, all those who adhere to them" (47). Similarly, William James, in his lesser known definition of religion, describes a separation of the visible and the invisible worlds, which parallels the separation between sacred and profane: "Religion has meant many things in human history: but when from now onward I use the word I mean to use it in the supernaturalist sense, as declaring that the so-called order of nature, which constitutes this world's experience, is only one portion of the total universe, and that there stretches beyond this visible world an unseen world of which we now know nothing positive, but in its relation to which the true significance of our present mundane life consists. A man's religious faith . . . means for me essentially his faith in the existence of an unseen order of some kind in which the riddles of the natural order may be found explained" (James 1956, 51). And if we believe in the existence of the unseen world, then religion as a social institution is for us the mediator between the invisible supernatural world and the visible, human and natural world; but that institution, with the behaviors tied to it, does not exist without the belief in the supernatural. "It is the premise of every religion—and this premise is religion's defining characteristic—that souls, supernatural beings, and supernatural forces exist. Furthermore, there are certain minimal categories of behavior, which, in the context of the *supernatural premise*, are always found in association with one another and which are the substance of religion itself" (Wallace 1966, 52). Following Wallace, I will use the presence of the supernatural premise as my touchstone for defining certain human behaviors as religious.

What is Unique to Religious Actions?

There is no intrinsically religious meaning in anything. Any object, person, time, or place, may become imbued with holiness and thus gain religious meaning. Religious actions are defined solely by their relation to the psychological realm of holiness. Holiness is a realm of content, psychological content, not psychological function or structure. Religious rituals have the capacity to induce ecstasy or at least excitement in the participants. This ecstasy can objectively be defined as measurable physiological arousal, but such arousal is not unique to religious occasions and cannot be regarded as identifying religious activities. There is no objective difference between physiological (and psychological) arousal during a religious ceremony and similar arousal during a Rolling Stones concert. The differences may be in the stimulus. Emotional arousal may seem like the most "objective" basis for a psychological definition of religion, but it be clear that this is not a unique aspect of religious actions.

Religions not only state the supernatural premise in an abstract general way, but also present many specific and elaborate ideas about the supernatural world and its inhabitant entities. Religious belief systems include also a philosophical anthropology (the "nature of man"), tied but not limited to the supernatural world, and psychological claims regarding human beings in this world. These claims most often refer to the existence of a soul, and less often to human "free will." As Tylor (1871) has suggested, the theory of the soul offers an explanation for two questions that puzzled primitive science: what happens to consciousness during sleep? what happens to consciousness after death? There is, of course, no necessary logical connection between the psychological part of religious beliefs (i.e., belief in free will and the soul) and the supernatural part. It may be possible to separate the two parts of the system, to believe in the soul or in free will without believing in the world of spirits. The idea of the soul is usually tied to the idea of immortality. The soul is immortal and survives physical death; this claim of religion is one of the most important, culturally and individually. As William James put it: "Religion, in fact, for the great majority of our own race, *means* immortality, and nothing else" (1961, 406).

The Task of Psychology

Religion seems to be an ideal subject matter for the psychologist. A system defined solely by the existence of beliefs and fantasies, which is a unique product of human cognitive capacities and a reflection of human flexibility and creativity, should be of great interest to psychologists. The basic question for the psychologist of religion is how to explain the existence of religious beliefs, their sources and their cultural manifestations, using psychological concepts, that is, concepts dealing with the mental abilities and processes of human beings.

It is quite readily assumed that psychology does not and cannot offer explanations for every manifestation of religion as a human activity. Other disciplines may be called upon to offer explanations for various aspects of religion.

Psychology, as a branch of systematic human knowledge, has two components: (a) a set of problems, topics, or questions, and (b) a range of methods by which these are investigated. The psychology of religion, in relation to other areas of psychology, can be defined through (a), its set of problems, which separates it from the rest of psychology. If the psychology of religion is viewed from the perspective of other disciplines dealing with religion, then the definition of the area is slightly different. What is the task of the psychology of religion and what answers does it have to provide? What is it about religion that cannot be answered by other disciplines? One definition of the psychology of religion may be negative; i.e., it will include those issues not dealt with by other disciplines. As this study will reveal, issues do not define themselves according to the boundaries among disciplines.

The question that the psychology of religion attempts to answer is the question of religious motives. Why do people engage in religious acts? Why does a particular individual engage in religious acts? These are the questions put before the psychologist of religion, as distinguished from the questions put before the historian or the sociologist of religion. Although the boundaries between any two disciplines studying religion may become irrelevant or may become a hindrance to pursuing many significant questions, each has distinctive contributions to make toward a larger understanding of religious experience. Religion as a phenomenon has been studied by history, sociology, philosophy, and anthropology, and the work done in all of these disciplines should be relevant to work in the psychology of religion. One significant difference between the study of religion in the traditional human science disciplines and the work done in psychology is that the traditional disciplines are historical, while modern academic psychology is not.

2

HISTORICAL BACKGROUND

Paraphrasing the cliché popular with writers of psychology textbooks, the relationship between psychology and religion is that between a young science and an old tradition. The rise of systematic psychology as an independent discipline has been correlated, and not by accident, with the decline of religion. This statement summarizes best what has happened over the past two hundred years. When discussing the psychological aspects of modernization, Inkeles and Smith (1974) note that "religion ranks with the extended family as the institution most often identified both as an obstacle to economic development and as a victim of the same process" (21). The process of modernization in the Third World in the twentieth century may be regarded as paralleling the scientific and industrial revolutions in the Western world in earlier centuries. In both cases religion can be seen retreating before the advancing forces of industrialization and science, but in both cases religion is not completely wiped out. The process of the decline of religion and the rise of science has been eloquently described by Frazer: "For ages the army of spirits, once so near, has been receding farther and farther from us, banished by the magic wand of science from hearth and home" (Frazer 1951, 633). The course of the struggle between science and religion is unidirectional and consistent. As Wallace (1966) states, "In these contests, whenever the battle is fully joined, and both parties commit themselves to the struggle, science *always* wins."

Secularization, the decline of religion as a social institution, has been connected with the rise of science. For the past five hundred years, religion has been dealt severe blows by the developing sciences. Natural sciences have been assaulting religion's traditional cosmology since the days of Giordano Bruno and Galileo, and biological sciences have demolished its view of man in the natural world. But it was left to the social sciences and psychology to examine the nature of religious beliefs, their development and their relativity, and in this way to deal what is probably the final blow to the credibility of religious claims (Cattell 1938). The historical development of academic disciplines parallels the effects of those disciplines on religion. If the challenge to religion started with the natural sciences in their progress, it has continued with the challenges from the social sciences and psychology, and the latter may be more serious and more systematic than the former. The decline of religion is especially tied to the rise of the social sciences, which examine the social order, often legitimized by religion. The insights of Auguste Comte and Emile Durkheim are useful in understanding the relationship between a declining religion and the rise of disciplines which are ready to look at the foundations of the social order. The social sciences have very clearly followed the Comtian model of the replacement of religious traditions by a new, rational and systematic science. The rise of the natural sciences constituted a well-documented threat to religion by challenging its cosmological and physical claims. This rise of the social sciences and psychology constituted an even more serious threat by exposing the psychological and relative nature of religious beliefs.

The social sciences are a threat to religion because they take religion as an object of study, and not as a representation of a special reality or a special mode of knowledge. All social sciences (indeed all human sciences) are a threat to religion, inasmuch as they study changes in culture over time and space and show time and again that beliefs and customs, including religious ones, are relative and culturally conditioned (Glock and Stark 1965). Psychology, as the discipline that deals directly with the nature of human beliefs, presents a most direct threat. Psychology is a challenge to religion in two ways: in challenging and rejecting the psychological notions of the soul and free will, which are part and parcel of religious tradition; and by being a part of the historical rise of science, a rise which challenges the supernatural premise and makes it less and less tenable. In other words, science is part of secularization, and psychology is tied to the historical rise of science. The kind of thinking which gave rise to modern science and to the discipline of psychology is inimical to the holding of the supernatural premise. Specific discoveries of modern science have undermined specific cosmological claims of religion, which started the long decline of religious beliefs. The war between religion and natural science as the prologue to the war between psychology and religion was ably described by Cattell (1938).

The rise of psychology represents an important part of the process of secularization. It represents the decline in the belief in the existence of the soul, a psychological theory which has been a part of every religious tradition. Modern psychology, as Allport stated (1950), is rather proud of being "a psychology without a soul," thus representing a direct departure from religious tradition. Actually, the development of modern psychology would not have been possible without rejecting the idea of the soul. The development of a scientific psychology has meant the naturalization and secularization of the soul, and finally its disappearance (Kantor 1969).

Paralleling the historical process of secularization, there is the process of the psychologizing of religion. Religion is becoming more psychological (or psychologistic) in two senses. In the first sense, religion has come to emphasize personal experience and personal faith rather than communal experiences or meanings. It is the individual who is being offered salvation in modern religion (and in modern psychology; cf. Beit-Hallahmi 1974b), rather than the community or society as a whole. Religion has become an individual matter, with its tenets becoming more abstract. Rather than clear cosmological claims and the promise of world transformation, religion now offers the believers notions of individual psychological change. The second sense in which religion is becoming psychologized is that of the rapprochement with applied and clinical psychology, which will be discussed below.

In historical perspective, the effects of religion on psychology seem obvious and preeminent. Psychology is the successor to religion in both scientific functions and social functions. Primitive theories of consciousness had been a part of religion until they were replaced by modern psychology. In their social and applied functions, modern psychological theories have acted to provide individuals with a secular meaning system, filling the "ecological niche" emptied by the decline of religion. Religion and psychology have become competing, alternative meaning systems for many individuals today. It has been noted that individuals in need of advice on personal difficulties tend to turn first to clergymen, rather than to the secular "helping professionals" (Gurin, Veroff, and Feld 1960). The competition between religion and psychology as meaning systems as expressed in the scholarly work of psychologists will be described below.

The Psychological Study of Religion: Historical Perspective

The history of the psychological study of religion is complex and paradoxical. It would be wrong to suggest that the phenomenon of religion has been neglected by psychology. Some of the best minds in the history of psychology have devoted considerable amounts of intellectual energy to the subject matter of religion, including Wundt (1916), Hall (1904), Freud (1927), Watson (1924), Skinner (1953), Cattell (1938), Maslow (1964), James (1902), Mowrer (1961), and Guntrip (1968). Wilhelm Wundt is universally considered the father of the laboratory paradigm in psychology, but he was also an early pioneer of the psychology of culture and the psychology of religion, and his *Volkerpsychologie* included three volumes on religion and mythology.

What is most often noted in discussions of the history of the psychological study of religion is that the area enjoyed a period of much activity and attention at the end of the nineteenth century and at the beginning of the twentieth (Beit-Hallahmi 1974a) and then declined greatly in terms of research activity and publications. We are able to speak of a "psychology of religion" movement, existing roughly between 1880 and 1930, whose history is enlightening and important for what has heppened to the psychological study of religion since then.

THE "PSYCHOLOGY OF RELIGION" MOVEMENT

During the last decade of the nineteenth century and the first quarter of this one, American psychologists were the pioneers and the leaders of the "psychology of religion" movement (Pratt 1908; Schaub 1922, 1924, 1926a, 1926b; Page, 1951). We will analyze the rise and fall of the study of religion as an acceptable topic in American academic psychology and will suggest possible explanation and implications. Beginning in the middle 1890s books and articles dealing with religious behavior became a frequent and welcome sight on the American psychological scene. *The American Journal of Psychology* and later *The Psychological Bulletin*, which started in 1904 and had regular annual reviews of the psychology of religion, published most of the articles and served as the mouthpieces of the new movement. The first study of conversion was published in 1896 (Leuba 1896), and three years later the first book to bear the title *The Psychology of Religion*

(Starbuck 1899) was published. This title was to become very popular in the ensuing thirty years. In 1902 James published his epoch-making *The Varieties of Religious Experience*, which gave another impetus to the movement. The word "psychology" and its various derivatives became common in the titles of books dealing with religion around that time.

Schaub (1924), describing the movement, wrote: "In the psychology of religion American scholars were the pioneers; and they have throughout remained in the vanguard of progress" (115). "When we consider such problems as conversion, revival phenomena, normal religious growth, or the influence of adolescence upon religious life, the American primacy is indisputable" (117). Psychology of religion as a field was started in the United States, as were most fields of psychology. Academic psychology became better developed in the United States than anywhere else in the world.

As we study the literature of the era, four names stand out. Two of them are those who gave the theoretical impetus and practical encouragement: G. S. Hall and W. James. Two others did most of the work and took over the leadership from the first generation: J. H. Leuba and E. D. Starbuck. William James is usually credited with most of the influence on the psychological study of religion in the United States, following publication of his *Varieties* in 1902. A closer scrutiny of the historical facts reveals that G. S. Hall was more instrumental than James in bringing about psychological studies of religion. Hall's students Leuba and Starbuck were the real pioneers, publishing their studies in the 1890s, before the "revival" caused by the publication of *Varieties* in 1902.

J. B. Pratt, in an article published in the heyday of the movement, (Pratt 1908) describes G. S. Hall as the guiding influence in this area, being the founder of the "Clark school of religious psychology." Early in the 1880s Hall began lecturing and writing on the "moral and religious training of children and adolescents" as part of his general interest in developmental problems. The publication of his article on the subject in 1882 marked the beginning of the new movement. Hall provided both encouragement for empirical studies as a teacher and testable hypotheses as a scholar. His interest in adolescence brought about empirical studies of religious "conversion," which became the most popular subject for such studies. Conversion was studied, among others, by Leuba (1896), Starbuck (1899), Coe (1916), Clark (1929), and Hall himself (1904). The pioneering journal established by G. S.

Hall in 1904 under the title *American Journal of Religious Psychology and Education* appeared in four volumes from May 1904 until July 1911. It was then continued as the *Journal of Religious Psychology, Including Its Anthropological and Sociological Aspects*, which was issued for three years, beginning with 1912, as a quarterly, but then only irregularly until 1915.

J. H. Leuba (1868–1946) was the most active among Hall's students. His numerous articles, most of them in the *Psychological Bulletin*, and his books (Leuba 1896, 1901, 1912, 1916, 1917, 1926a, 1926b, 1934) gave him the leadership position in the movement as long as it existed. Born in Switzerland, he came to the United States as a young man and studied at Clark University under G. Stanley Hall. In 1895, he graduated from Clark University and became a fellow there, and in 1896 he published the first study of conversion in academic psychology. Later on he moved to Bryn Mawr College, where he spent all his active academic life.

Leuba is responsible for the classical study on religious beliefs among scientists and psychologists (1916). He found that more eminent scientists were more likely than other scientists to profess no religious beliefs. The same finding held for psychologists. It is not surprising that Leuba reports this finding, because he was a critic of religion, a sceptic writing about other sceptics. In his book on religious mysticism, he emphasized the importance of sexual impulses and sexual symbolism in religious rituals and in religious ecstasy. Leuba has been described as empiricistic, reductionistic, and antireligious. There is no doubt that in his time he was the least inclined among the leading psychologists to pay respects to conventional religion.

As Leuba himself reported, his early experiences in Switzerland led him to his critical views regarding religion and religious people. Raised in a Calvinist environment, he became a doubter and then had a conversion experience induced by the Salvation Army. Later on his studies of science made him into an atheist. He remained, through the rest of his life, a critic of religion very much in the same vein as Freud, but more than that, he became a critic of religious hypocrites. He accused G. S. Hall and others of hypocrisy when they kept up the appearance of religiosity for the sake of their social standing, or for the sake of keeping the "ignorant masses" under control. The current standing of Leuba's contribution can be directly gauged by the fact that of the six books he authored during his lifetime, four are still in print, and one of them (*The Psychology of Religious Mysticism*) has been reissued in 1972. This is no mean accomplishment, and is a real tribute to one man's work. His ideas regarding the origins of religion and magic are reminiscent of those proposed by Freud and Malinowski, and their brilliance should keep Leuba numbered among the true greats of the study of religion.

E. D. Starbuck (1866–1947) was born in Indiana, to a devout Quaker farming family. After undergraduate work at Indiana University, Starbuck went on to Harvard University, where he received his M.A. in 1895, and then to Clark University, where he studied under G. S. Hall and received his Ph.D. in 1897. In 1890 he was stirred by Max Muller's *Introduction to the Science of Religion* and decided to start studying religion. In 1893, at Harvard University, he circulated two questionnaires, one on conversion and the other on "gradual growth" in religion. In 1894 and 1895 he presented papers on his research before the Harvard Religious Union. After graduating from Clark University, he remained there as a fellow in the late 1890's, together with Leuba. Starbuck's 1899 book, *The Psychology of Religion*, was based on studies started at Harvard under James and continued at Clark under Hall. He had the support and encouragement of James in his work. As Starbuck himself reports in a frank autobiographical statement, there was some tension in his relationship with Hall, and mutual criticism is much in evidence. His teaching positions included high school teaching in Indiana (1890–91), teaching mathematics at Vincennes University in Indiana (1891–93), teaching education at Earlham College (1904–06), teaching philosophy (1906–30) at the State University of Iowa, and teaching philosophy (1930–38) and psychology (1938–43) at the University of Southern California. If we look at Starbuck's list of publications, we discover that among his eleven books only one, *The Psychology of Religion* (1899), was devoted to the psychology of religion. This volume enjoyed three editions and was reprinted several times. It was also translated into German in 1909. After the turn of the century, Starbuck devoted most of his creative energy to "character training" and devised selections of fairy-tales, novels, and biographies which would contribute to the moral education of the young.

Starbuck's lasting contribution is his early survey of conversion cases, summarized in his Ph.D. thesis, several articles, and the book *The Psychology of Religion*. This work was immortalized by James when he used Starbuck's data in the *Varieties of Religious Experience*. While the basic findings of the survey have been accepted and seem to fit with classical and modern notions of conversion, the theoretical construction seems hopelessly naive today. Together with Hall, Starbuck regards conversion as an adolescent phenomenon and has the data to show it. His findings are still quoted today and are beyond dispute, but his psychology and his definition of religion as an "instinct" cannot be taken seriously. Starbuck's studies of conversion and his views about religion in general tend to reflect the zeitgeist and parallel those of James and Hall. Starbuck's attitude toward religion was clearly positive, and he stresses the importance of the psychology of religion as contributing to religious education. According to James (1899), Starbuck's aim in starting his research in the psychology of religion was to bring about reconciliation in the feud between science and religion. According to Starbuck's autobiographical account (1937), his interest in religion was very much an attempt to answer, via systematic study, both doubts and curiosities about religion. If we attempt an evaluation of Starbuck's work from the perspective of several generations, we might conclude that it will be remembered more by historians of the field than by practitioners. While Starbuck's prominence was already recognized by his contemporaries, succeeding generations have remembered him primarily because of his pioneering surveys of conversion and because of his association with James. Future generations will remember him for being the first to use the term "psychology of religion," which has gone on to become so popular since the turn of the century. His work may belong with the classics of the field, but even among scholars, it is likely to remain a classic that is seldom read.

E. S. Conklin was another member of the "Clark school of religious psychology." He studied under Hall and graduated from Clark in 1911 later becoming head of the psychology department of the University of Oregon. His book *The Psychology of Religious Adjustment* (1929) was the swan's song of the group's activity, together with the books by E. T. Clark (1929) and G. Betts (1929). J. B. Pratt (1907, 1920) can be regarded as one of W. James's followers in the study of religion.

EXPLAINING THE RISE OF THE MOVEMENT

In an article published in 1924 (Schaub 1924) the rise of the movement was described in a way that gives some insight into the zeitgeist that produced it: "The dawn of the twentieth century witnessed the rise of a new approach to the study of religion . . . psychological investigations along strictly empirical and scientific lines" (113). As we go back to Starbuck (1899) in the first book dedicated exclusively to the psychology of religion, this positivistic approach becomes even clearer: "Science has conquered one field after another, until it is now entering the most complex, the most inaccessible and, of all, the most sacred domain—that of religion" (1). The psychology of religion movement was undoubtedly influenced by the growth in the academic study of religion in the nineteenth century, and by the rise of the history of religions and comparative religion as academic "movements." Philosophy has always dealt with questions of belief and religion. Psychology, as a legitimate heir and descendant of philosophy, took upon itself the chore of objectively studying subjects that formerly belonged to philosophy. The pioneers of the empirical-experimental approach to human behavior saw religion as a subject fit to study, and they eagerly wanted to prove that even this area of study can be studied "scientifically." Great advances were being made in the sociology of religion and anthropology. Studies of primitive religion by Frazer and Tylor aroused much interest and theorizing. Given this background, the pioneers in the movement felt that the time was right for a positivistic approach to religion in psychology. Another important factor was the basic positive attitude to religion, as reflected in the above quotation. Together with faith in the scientific spirit, there was also a profound respect for religion as a human and social enterprise.

Following the traditional view of religion as something necessary to human society, the references to religion itself in the writings of W. James, G. S. Hall, J. H. Leuba and E. D. Starbuck show this attitude of deference to and reverence for basic religious dogmas. Publication of psychological articles in religious and theological journals shows the spirit of cooperation and contribution to religion that prevailed in the movement. Schaub (1924) claims that to the influence of the psychology of religion "may be traced much of what is most distinctive in the religious thought, as well as most fruitful and promising in the religious aspirations and procedure, of the past generation" (114).

THE DECLINE OF THE MOVEMENT

The rapid decline and final demise of the movement were reflected in the disappearance of the annual reviews of the psychology of religion field that had been published in the *Psychological Bulletin*. Since 1904, though more particularly beginning with its issue of June 1909, the *Psychological Bulletin* has carried reviews of publications in the psychology of religion. The area of "the psychology of belief" was also covered in some volumes. The decline in the area was reflected in the fact that no reviews were published between the years 1928 and 1933. The last review (Cronbach 1933) contained mostly material taken from German and French sources, showing the loss of interest in the area in the United States. Since 1933 the term "psychology of religion" has been rarely mentioned in the pages of the *Psychological Bulletin,* which once was the movement's mouthpiece.

A survey on courses in psychology offered by undergraduate colleges published in 1938 (Henry 1938) showed the decline of interest in this area, compared with the previous decade (cf. Schaub 1924). Out of 154 colleges surveyed, only twenty-four offered psychology of religion courses. Thus, a little over three decades after its birth, the psychology of religion movement was dead.

Douglas (1963) offered the following reasons for its decline:

1. The psychology of religion failed to separate itself from theology, philosophy of religion, and the general dogmatic and evangelistic tasks of religious institutions.
2. In the desperate effort to be recognized as "scientific," there was an emphasis on collecting discrete facts without integrating them into a comprehensive theory.
3. The use of data collection methods and explanations was often uncritical and incompetent.
4. The climate of public opinion was changing, away from religion and toward a behavioristic and positivistic world view.
5. The study of religion was conflictual for both researcher and subject, because of their own personal investment in religion.
6. "Subjective" phenomena were avoided by developing social science, which tried to be "empirical" and "objective."

Strunk (1957) regarded the following factors as crucial:

1. Theological interest in the field introduced speculative and apologetic tendencies, which hampered advancement.
2. Psychoanalytic approaches to the study of religion attracted more attention and efforts, since they seemed more promising.
3. The influence of behaviorism led to the neglect of complex human behaviors as the focus of attention in academic psychology.

As illustrated above, the philosophical-theological approach could not have gained much respect for the psychology of religion area among younger, more critical scholars. Despite the publication of several impressive studies (Starbuck 1897; Leuba 1896, 1916; Coe, 1916), such a naive theoretical approach limited the impact of the movement on general psychology and separated it from the mainstream of academic research. Inside academic psychology in the 1920s and 1930s, interest in religious behavior began to be perceived as evidence of unscientific orientation. The theoretical and ideological basis of the movement showed that the psychology of religion was basically a residue of the philosophical tradition in psychology. This was probably the most severe limitation of the movement, which ultimately caused its decline.

The contribution of psychoanalysis was a mixed blessing to the psychology of religion. On the one hand, it was the source of many stimulating ideas in regard to religion, but, on the other hand, it never generated conventional academic research, nor did it penetrate academic departments. In addition to the reasons suggested above, some other factors can be identified. One is the growth and development of other areas of academic psychology, introducing new fads which won interest, energy, and students. Another may be social pressure, or lack of support from the outside. The book by Thurstone and Chave (1929) signified a new stage in the development of social psychology and coincided with the decline in the psychology of religion area. Objective methods of attitude measurement gave a new boost to the area of studying social and political behavior. Social psychology might have incorporated the study of religious attitudes into its realm and thus transferred the study of religion into a new stage, but this did not happen.

The issue of social pressure is rarely discussed in connection with the psychology of religion. However, as Glock and Stark (1965) show, any serious systematic study of religion must be a threat to religious institutions. The threat posed by the psychology of religion movement was responded to by taking it over. The second generation of workers in the movement (such as Pratt, Coe, Ames, and Johnson), as Strunk (1957) points outs, were religionists first and psychologists second.

In another interpretation of the decline of the movement, Homans (1970) states that this decline " . . . coincided with the beginnings of both theological existentialism and psychoanalysis" (99). Another coincidence pointed out by Homans (1970) is the one between the appearance of pastoral psychology and the decline of the movement. Homans suggests that the pastoral counseling process is the heir to the conversion experience described by the psychologists of religion.

It is clear that neutralizing the threat of the movement by taking it under the wings of religious institutions had a significant role in its decline and stagnation. No sinister, deliberate conspiracy is implied here. The movement was not an unwilling victim, since its friendliness to religion was widely proclaimed. The whole takeover process was a rather natural one, a combination of inherent weakness and external pressure. Pastoral counseling is thus the natural and only successor to the psychology of religion movement.

Another important social factor that seems to influence psychologists is what is called here "the ivory tower effect." As early as 1916 it was shown that scientists, and especially psychologists, are less religious than most of the American population (Leuba 1916, 1934). More recent studies show the same phenomenon (Stark 1963). Since academic communities in general are less religious than most of the population, social scientists acquire the impression that religion is "neutralized" (Adorno et al. 1950). This misconception may have contributed to the declining academic interest in religion. Scientists in the 1930s might have felt that the long war between science and religion was won by science, and there was not much left to study in religion.

As the discussion above indicates, it was a combination of inherent, internal weaknesses, and the existence of outside pressures, that caused the decline in the acceptability of religion as a focus for psychological inquiry. One possible inference is that internal weaknesses, mainly the lack of a nonreligious, nonphilosophical theoretical basis doomed the movement from its inception and caused its early death. At the same time outside pressures, both within and without academic psychology, were considerable. The movement was obviously an easy prey, and its demise was quick and total. The years between 1930 and 1960 were a low point (or the "dark ages") for publications dealing with psychology and religion. Allport (1950) pointed out the interesting change in the status of religion and sex as appropriate subjects of study between 1930 and 1960: during those thirty years sex became a very fashionable area of research, while religion became almost a taboo subject. Since 1960, there has been a mild "revival" of psychological writings dealing with religion.

Religion's Response to Psychology

Two leading researchers in the sociology of religion, Glock and Stark (1965) state that social science research is " . . . putting religion on the defensive about some of its traditional beliefs and the effect, in the long run, is likely to produce a process of accommodation parallel to that which religion experienced in its earlier confrontation with the natural sciences" (291). The effects of the rise of psychology as a discipline and the rise of systematic secular psychological theories on the institution of religion can be viewed at three levels. First, the rise of psychology is part of the general challenge of modern science to religion. Second, it is a part of the rise of modern social science and modern social critiques, exemplified in the work of Marx, Durkheim, and Freud. Third, there are the specific effects of psychology as an emerging scientific discipline and as an emerging technology.

THEOLOGICAL RESPONSES
Psychoanalysis is the one development in modern psychological theories that has received most attention from theologians. Homans (1970) analyzes the reaction of major Protestant theologians to psycho-analytic ideas. There is a voluminous literature of theological responses to psychoanalysis, both Catholic and Protestant, which can best be described as attempting a reconciliation, or a compromise, with Freud's ideas (see Beit-Hallahmi 1978). "Liberal" Protestant theology in the twentieth century has been using depth psychology and "humanistic" psychology approaches, and psychological concepts have become part of the theological discourse. Theologians have become amazingly fluent in the language of psychoanalysis, in its various dialects from Freud to Erikson, and in the language of client centered psychotherapy (Homans 1968a). While specific references to psychological writings are to be found mainly in liberal theology, the process of psychologizing religion is occurring also among the conservative branches of organized religion. All branches of popular theology, presented not in scholarly publications but through the mass media, especially television, offer the believers a personal and psychological kind of salvation. Religious salvation today is defined in psychological and temporal ways, such as "peace of mind" and happiness. There is less emphasis on everlasting life or the kingdom of heaven, and more on the private and personal. It is significant that popular proselytizing in the United States today is based on "accepting Jesus as your personal savior." The benefits of religion to the faithful are presented as personal and immediate. There is an obvious continuity between secular psychotherapy, with its message of private solutions to private problems, and the contemporary religious message of private salvation

(Beit-Hallahmi 1974b, 1976). The psychologizing of religion in this sense is not only a response to psychology but a reflection of the parallel roles of both religion and secular psychotherapy in social control (Beit-Hallahmi 1976).

THE RISE OF PASTORAL PSYCHOLOGY

One reaction by the religious establishment to the early development of psychological approaches to religion was the pastoral counseling movement, in existence since the 1930s. It has been a reaction to both academic approaches and applied approaches in psychology. Pastoral counseling has sought to appropriate the techniques of secular psychotherapy and integrate them into the work of the clergy.

From the viewpoint of the history of the "helping professions," pastoral counseling has been a part of the movement for nonmedical psychotherapy. From the perspective presented by Glock and Stark (1956), the development of pastoral counseling can be seen as part of the process of accommodation and assimilation, through which religion responds to technological and scientific innovations. Pastoral counseling was not just a reaction to a new technology, but also a response to specific psychological theories. Pastoral psychology has been specifically influenced by psychoanalysis, including neo-Freudian theories, and to some extent by client centered theory in counseling (Homans 1970). Homans states that " . . . the first theological attempt to deal with psychoanalysis was made by pastoral psychology" (15).

Thus, the pastoral psychology movement represents one reaction of institutional religion to the challenge presented by secularization in general and psychology in particular. Its growth and development are visible in several trends in clerical practice. It gave a new content to the role of the clergy, which made the competition from secular psychology easier to deal with. By incorporating secular techniques into his work, the clergyman became just as "good" as (and cheaper than) the secular therapist. Counseling became a major component of the professional training of clergy. Historically, the rise of pastoral counseling was tied to the "mental hygiene" movement and to the widespread development of nonmedical psychotherapy. The clergyman is an ideal candidate for effective intervention; he is part of the community, and is involved in crisis situations as part of his role. People have always come to clergymen for advice. The challenge facing the pastors was that their advice was losing credibility with the parishioners. By integrating the traditional religious answers in times of crisis with secular notions, the pastoral role became more credible and more effective. The development of pastoral psychology and pastoral counseling helps religion and professional religionists in gaining and maintaining credibility.

The journal *Pastoral Psychology*, which appeared between 1950 and 1972, is the best written record of the pastoral psychology movement in the years of its greatest popularity. The list of contributors to its first volume included such prominent psychologists and psychiatrists as Molly Harrower, Rollo May, Carl R. Rogers, Karen Horney, O. Spurgeon English, William C. Menninger, Lawrence S. Kubie, Franz Alexander, Karl A. Menninger, and Erich Fromm. The dominant spirit of the volume can best be described as the progeny of a marriage between liberal Christian theology and liberal psychoanalysis, characterized by considerable sophistication in pyschoanalytic terms, a liberal stand on many issues of the day, and a large dose of positive thinking. Actually, the pastoral psychology movement can be viewed as an integral part of the Americanization of psychoanalysis.

The institutionalization of pastoral psychology is one area where the impact of psychology on religion is rather substantial. What it means in practice is that most of the clergy in the English-speaking world today have been exposed to psychological theories as part of their training, first through theology and to a larger extent through formal training in pastoral counseling. While the impact of psychology is more dominant in liberal theology, both liberal and traditional denominations train their clergy in pastoral psychology. While it is true that conservative denominations use psychology for counseling techniques and not for theology, the effects of psychology are clearly felt even in those groups.

THE IMPACT OF PSYCHOLOGY ON RELIGIOUS STUDIES

What are the academic reflections of religion as an institution? In the United States today, the academic side of religion has two aspects: religious studies and theology. While departments of religious studies have come into existence in quite a few universities and serve as the home for scholarly work on religion, theology is not considered as a legitimate academic discipline outside of religious institutions.

Theology exists as part of the institution of religion, while the history of religions, as a discipline, is part of the secular world of academic scholarship. The discernible effects of psychological theories on theology and on organized religion have been reviewed above. The question now is whether we can assess the influence of psychology on the work of scholars in other disciplines who are studying religion. The answer seems to be that the situation of psychology in relation to the academic study of religion is the same as that of psychology in relation to the humanities and social sciences in general. Any scholar in the humanities today is familiar with psychological concepts and theories, mainly those of depth psychology. There has been a historical trend for the greater use of psychological ideas in the traditional humanities, such as history and literature, and there have been attempts to formalize a new discipline of psychohistory. All of these developments affect scholars who study religion. The criticisms directed at the uses (and abuses) of psychology in the humanities in general also apply to the uses of psychology in the humanities when the subject matter is religion. Students of comparative religion and the history of religion are familiar with psychological interpretations of their materials, but quite often react to them critically. The methodological issues here are similar to those which come up in the psychological study of religion, and will be discussed below.

3

IDEOLOGICAL AND PERSONAL APPROACHES TO THE PSYCHOLOGY OF RELIGION

Any discipline studying religion is forced into dealing with the validity of religious claims, and that is because religion does make rather strong and unusual claims, which often enjoy a privileged status within the individual scholar's own culture. The attitude of the psychologist toward the claims of religion does have a bearing on the way it is going to be studied. Religious psychologists treat their subject matter differently than do their nonreligious colleagues, because they accord a special status to religious claims, religious institutions, and individual experiences in religion. The difference in approach between religious and nonreligious psychologists can be illusrated by an analogy to Marxism. We do expect a difference between Marxist and non-Marxist studies of Marxism. The Marxist student of Marxism will admit its similarity to other ideologies, without casting doubts on its validity. A look at the personal history and education of most of the contributors to the study of religion shows that they are, in many cases, from a religious background, which often included seminary education. This introduces another kind of personal involvement, and creates a situation today in which those who study religion are committed to it, while those who are not show little interest in the area or sometimes even a slight disdain. This imbalance creates an obvious problem in terms of basic theoretical perspective. The dominant perspective appears to be based on an interest in the preservation of religion as a social institution. The belief that religion is a positive force in individual and social life is central to this approach. Although most psychologists are not committed to religion, either as a personal belief or as a topic of study, there exists a minority who are, and they are the ones responsible for most of the activity in the psychology of

32

religion. As a result, we may have today primarily a religious psychology of religion.

The Study of Religion and the Religious Beliefs of Psychologists

The finding that scientists and academicians are less religious than the rest of the population has been amply documented (Argyle and Beit-Hallahmi 1975). Even those who found that academicians were not totally divorced from religiosity described them as adhering to a most secularized kind of religious creed (Faulkner and DeJong 1972).

Stark (1963) has provided a convincing illustration of the incompatibility of the scholarly ethos and religion, and also pointed to the lack of productivity on the part of religious scholars. What has been presumed to be incompatible with the religious stance has been designed by various authors as the "scientific," "scholarly," or "intellectual" viewpoint (Campbell and Magill 1968; Knapp and Greenbaum 1953; Lazarsfeld and Thielens 1958; Stark 1963; MacDonell and Campbell 1971). The presumed incompatibility between the scientific orientation and the religious one is supported by the fact that sectarian schools generally rank lower with respect to the quality of their educational programs, student ability, and faculty productivity (Trent 1967; Pattillo and Mackenzie 1966; Hassenger 1967). The explanation for this is that religious commitment leads to a compromising of scholarly standards.

Since academic communities are, in general, less religious than most of the population, social scientists have the impression that religion is "neutralized." The "ivory tower effect" is part of what Anderson (1968a, 1968b) has described as the intellectual subsociety, transethnic and transreligious. Steinberg (1973) reports that the religious composition of faculty members in higher education is markedly different from that of the general population. Catholics are underrepresented while Jews are overrepresented among faculty members. The fact that Jewish faculty members tend to be concentrated in a relatively small group of institutions, most often of high quality, tends to make their influence more pronounced. It is not surprising that this subsociety will tend to minimize the importance of religious and ethnic factors.

While most studies agree on the fact that scientists and academicians tend to be less religious than the general population, more detailed investigations discovered differences in religiosity among academic disciplines. Lehman and Shriver (1968) introduced the concept of scholarly distance from religion as a predictor of religiosity among academicians. This concept refers to the extent to which an academic discipline considers religion a legitimate object of study. Thus, historians would be lower in scholarly distance than biologists because religion is an accepted subject for historians to study while for biologists it is not. Lehman and Shriver (1968) predicted that a greater degree of religious involvement would be found among academicians in the disciplines with this scholarly distance. Physicists and chemists were expected to be more religious than anthropologists, psychologists, and sociologists, and the findings supported this prediction.

These findings are especially relevant to the discussion of religious beliefs among psychologists. Psychology is, at least in principle, a "low distance" discipline, and its practitioners are likely to explore religion as they explore other human behaviors. Psychology, as a discipline, would prescribe an analytical stance toward religion, and thus would make it less likely for psychologists to be religiously committed. An identical prediction regarding the religiosity of psychologists can be made from the point of view of occupational psychology (Bordin 1966; Bordin, Nachmann, and Segal 1963). The choice of psychology as an occupation stems from an individual's strong need for the exploration of interpersonal and personal experiences. Scientific creativity requires skepticism and doubt (Bordin 1966), which in psychology include skepticism about beliefs and mores. The "debunking" effect of psychology, as a science which often finds that widely held ideas are empirically invalid, should have a reinforcing influence on the initial skepticism of those who decide to become psychologists.

Together with other social scientists, psychologists are considered unconventional, and with some justification (Bereiter and Freedman 1962; Roe 1956). This lack of conventionality coupled with the attitude of skepticism that the scientist displays towards social norms should be reflected in lower religious involvement. Studies of religious beliefs among psychologists tend to support the impression of relative irreligiosity. Leuba (1916) studied the religious beliefs of fifty "distinguished psychologists" and fifty-seven "lesser psychologists and historians." He reported that the proportion of believers in God among the distinguished psychologists was the lowest of all the groups studied (13.2%). The percentage of believers among the "lesser" psychologists was 32.1 and within the whole group was 24.2. These results were consistent with Leuba's hypothesis that religious personalities are less likely to be found among social scientists than among physical scientists. Very similar findings regarding psychologists and other scientists were reported by Rogers (1965).

Roe (1952) studied a group of fifty-four eminent scientists, including twenty-two psychologists and anthropologists. Most of the scientists came from a Protestant background, and a small minority were Jews. Only three members of the group were active in any church, and the rest were "indifferent" to religion. One clear limitation of the Roe study is that only eminent scientists and psychologists were included. On the other hand, their eminence may have something to do with the embodiment of traits crucial to the fulfillment of the academic psychologist's role. A confirmation of Roe's (1953) and Anderson's (1968a) findings came from McClelland (1964), who stated: "I can hardly think of a psychologist, sociologist, or anthropologist of my generation who would admit publicly or privately to a religious commitment of any kind . . ." (118).

Henry, Sims, and Spray (1971) studied a large group of mental health professionals—psychologists, psychiatrists, clinical psychologists, and social workers. Almost fifty percent of the clinical psychologists in this study described their "cultural affinity" as Jewish. In terms of religious affiliation, as differentiated from cultural affinity, twenty percent of the clinical psychologists identified themselves as Protestants, eight percent as Catholic, and thirty percent as Jewish. The rest reported various shades of nonreligiosity. This picture is, of course, striking when compared with national figures for religious affiliation. Henry et al. (1971) see it as part of the "social marginality" of all mental health professions (Szasz and Nemiroff 1963). This marginality is similar to that described by Anderson (1968a) for academicians in general; we have no reason to assume that nonpracticing clinical psychologists are different. Burtchaell (1970) stated that many of the most influential and capable social scientists have been Jews who felt antagonism toward religion and were reluctant to study it. This claim is especially significant in view of the findings by Steinberg (1973) quoted above. Ragan, Malony, and Beit-Hallahmi (1980) found that in a random sample of APA members forty-three percent reported a belief in a "transcendent deity," compared to ninety-eight percent of the general population. Of those APA members who reported a religious affiliation, fifty-one percent were Protestant (compared to sixty-nine percent in the American population), nineteen percent were Jewish (compared to almost three percent in the general population), and fifteen percent were Catholic (compared to twenty-five percent in the general population). This study again confirms that in both religious beliefs and religious affiliation, psychologists are far from representative of the general population, or "the real world."

Psychologists Who Study Religion

The findings on the indifferent or negative attitudes of most social scientists and psychologists toward religion and the lack of professional interest in it strongly suggest that those psychologists who are interested in religion as a topic of study would present a totally different picture. The stereotype of the psychologist who is interested in religion, at least among his academic colleagues, embodies the notion of strong religious commitments or frustrated theological ambitions. This stereotype, strangely enough, seems to have much truth to it. Ragan, Malony, and Beit-Hallahmi (1980) found that members of the APA who study religion tend to be religious themselves. A close or even superficial scrutiny of the personal histories, education, and writings of most of the contributors to the psychology of religion shows that they come, in most cases, from religious backgrounds. Their commitment to religion is clear (Allport 1950, 1978), and many of them see their main contribution in terms of helping religion become better and stronger (Dittes 1967). Many of them have been ordained as ministers or priests, and many are affiliated with divinity schools, theology schools or departments of religious studies. (This is also a reflection of the fact that divinity schools today are more hospitable to the psychology of religion than are psychology departments. Psychology department chairpersons looking for experts on the psychology of religion are rare indeed.)

It seems that in most cases, only a personal religious commitment will motivate a psychologist to break the strong norm against studying religion. Most psychologists of religion are religious, and in their cases personal involvement overrides disciplinary norms. Religious psychologists who study the psychology of religion do not regard such psychological endeavors as a threat. For them the warfare between religion and science is over, both personally and collectively. Studying religion "objectively" may even be a way of working through conflicts and finding justification for their beliefs.

Division 36 of the American Psychological Association, in existence since 1975 under the official title, "Psychologists Interested in Religious Issues" (PIRI), is the successor to the organization with the same name and represents the same interests. (Psychologists interested in Religious Issues, Inc., was the nondenominational successor to the American Catholic Psychological Association.) Without a great effort at textual analysis one must note that its name does not reflect religion as an object of study, but only "Religious Issues." The founders of the division are clearly committed religionists. The existence and the activities of the division tend to support the stereotype held by most academic psychologists about psychologists who are interested in religion as part of their professional activity. As we have seen, this stereotype accurately reflects reality. The Society for the Scientific Study of Religion (SSSR), an interdisciplinary nonsectarian organization, includes a minority of psychologists among its members, the majority of whom are sociologists, theologians, historians, and clergymen. Most of the well-known researchers in both the sociology and the psychology of religion are members of the SSSR. As suggested above, most SSSR members who are psychologists also have a background of religious education; some of these have even been ordained. The stereotype of the psychologist of religion as somebody who has a particular religious axe to grind seems to be largely justified. It is the domination of the psychology of religion by religious psychologists that makes most academic psychologists uneasy.

Searching in a university library for a book entitled *The Psychology of Religion,* the innocent reader is likely in most cases to find a volume which is more religious than psychological. The specific religious orientation can in most cases be simply deduced from the author's institutional affiliation and the publisher's identity. The religionists' contributions to the psychology of religion may contain useful insights, but they are hampered by the excess baggage of theology, which to most psychologists may seem strange or even bizarre. The theological language used by such authors is not likely to be shared with readers outside his particular tradition, while the psychological language may well be. Some of these books are scholarly, in the sense of demonstrating an excellent knowledge of psychological literature. However, the melange resulting from the combination of theology and psychology is likely to be exasperating for most psychologists. An example of such writing is the book by Oates (1973), which is a compendium of psychological theories and findings from a variety of sources, presented rather clearly and unsystematically, together with biblical quotations and theological assertions. Anybody who will try to make heads or tails of the book in search of a psychological theory will be sorely frustrated. Its religious message, however, is much clearer to grasp and is consistent with the fact that the author is a faculty member at the Southern Baptist Theological Seminary. Many of the psychologists involved in writing of this nature hold positions in religious institutions, and their commitment to religion is quite obvious.

Religious psychology presents religion from the inside, but is by necessity limited to one religious tradition, that of the presenter. However, these presentations produce documents which are of value as source materials, texts to be interpreted by students of religious traditions. Personal statements by psychologists who have been involved in writing in the area of psychology of religion (Malony 1978; Clark 1978; Dittes 1978; Gorsuch 1978; Strunk 1978) show quite clearly that a commitment to a religious viewpoint is an important part of the motivation for their work as psychologists. Religious psychologists do not ask the same questions as nonreligious psychologists, as long as they do not consider religion as an object of study. However, they may consider manifestations of religion as objects. A psychological approach to the phenomenon of religion implies less than full acceptance of the supernatural premise. Religious psychologists accept the supernatural premise and seek to specify its effects. Nonreligious psychologists do not accept the supernatural premise. Allport would be an example of the former; Freud, of the latter.

What we have today in the writings of psychologists about religion are really three separate traditions:

1. a religious psychology, which focuses on religious apologetics (e.g., Johnson 1959).
2. a psychology of religion, which focuses on the psychological explanation of religious phenomena (e.g., Spanos and Hewitt 1979).
3. a social psychology of religion, studying the social-psychological correlates of religion and religiosity, without taking a stand on the validity of religious claims (Beit-Hallahmi 1973b; Argyle and Beit-Hallahmi 1975).

The difference between a religious psychology and a psychology of religion is that between defending religious beliefs and explaining them. Psychology of religion treats religion as a phenomenon for systematic psychological study, while religious psychology aims at promoting religion through the adaptation and use of psychological concepts. Our division of the literature into religious psychology, psychology of religion, and the social psychology of religion is based on works rather than on individuals. It is not *ad hominem*. The same individual psychologists can be engaged in all three, though in reality this is not often the case. The same individual can contribute to religious psychology, to the psychology of religion, and to the social psychology of religion. Allport, for example, has contributed to all three areas of the literature. The literature of religious psychology can be identified by the inclusion of a differentiation between "good" religion and "bad" religion, presented under the psychological terms of neurotic vs. mature religion (Allport 1950) or intrinsic vs. extrinsixc religion (Allport and Ross 1967). Religious psychologists are preoccupied with the question of the positive and negative effects of religious beliefs and practices, and with the effects of religion on personality functioning. The latter can be seen as the legacy of Jamesian pragmatism and the functionalist school in psychology, together with the stand of the apologist. The differences in approaches between religious psychology, the psychology of religion, and the social psychology of religion can be best illustrated with a concrete example: The question of the correlation between religiosity and prejudice.

The history of research on the question of the relationship between religiosity and prejudice is quite well known (Argyle and Beit-Hallahmi 1975). There has been a great number of studies since 1945 showing that in the English speaking world there is usually a positive correlation between conventional religiosity and the holding of various social prejudices, e.g., racial prejudice. The way these findings have been interpreted provides us with a significant illustration for the differences between the religious and the irreligious approaches to the psychological study of religion. Religious psychologists reacted to the finding with disappointment, and they provided a distinction between those who are deeply religious and less prejudiced, and the majority of conventionally religious people, who are prejudiced (Allport and Ross 1967). Nonreligious psychologists have dealt with this question as part of the social psychology of religion by pointing to a variety of factors in religion as an institution and in society around it. Argyle and Beit-Hallahmi (1975) present a social-psychological view, which emphasizes the correlational nature of the findings and their social context.

The social-psychological view is that religion does not cause prejudice, but that religiosity is, in most cases, a part of the social-psychological complex which includes overall conventionality and conservatism. Thus, the social-psychological finding remains the same: church members are more prejudiced than nonchurch members for social reasons. Religious psychologists have put much effort into showing "good religion" is correlated with less prejudice, but "good religion" represents a small social minority, and so does not affect the general correlation.

Religious psychologists treat their subject matter differently because they accord a special status to religious claims, religious institutions, and individual experiences in religion. This has obviously affected the whole tenor of the psychology of religion field and has contributed to its difficulties. The religious psychologist will admit the similarity between religion and other belief systems but will also emphasize the correctness of religion.

In addition to apologetics in the defense of one's particular religion, there is also the phenomenon of apologetics in the defense of religion in general. This is a unique historical development, which has to be seen in its own context. It can be encountered most often in the United States, and it is a part of the American context. The ecumenical approach to apologetics is thoroughly American, and reflects very much the American, as opposed to the European, view of religion (Argyle and Beit-Hallahmi 1975). It is a defense of religion as a world view and as a general way of life, reflecting the notion that some religion is always better than no religion. The literature of apologetics via psychology or "religious psychology" of all kinds is in itself important as the subject matter of research for the psychologist, the sociologist, or the historian of religions.

Modern Apologetics: Psychoanalysis as the Stimulus

The literature of religious apologetics in relation to psychology, under a variety of headings, is enormous and complex. Apologetic literature on the psychology of religion, and especially on psychoanalysis, attempts to reconcile religious traditions and modern secular views. In the case of psychoanalysis, the job is objectively difficult, but not insurmountable for the true apologist. Psychoanalysis, as a general personality theory and within its specific treatment of religion, has been the stimulus to a flood of reactions from individual believers and religious institutions (Beit-Hallahmi 1978, 1983). There have been two kinds of reactions, one rejecting and the other apologetic. Thomas Merton (1948), for example, rejected psychoanalysis completely and denounced its basic approach. R. S. Lee (1948) found that Freud was totally wrong about religion, but his ideas on other subjects were actually supportive of Christian doctrine. A historical development that has contributed to the reduced role of psychoanalysis in contemporary psychology of religion has been the rise of an intellectual movement which aimed at reconciling religion and psychoanalysis. This movement of compromise tended to depreciate the importance of specific psychoanalytic interpretations in favor of more general discussions. One can easily point to the thousands of books and articles written by religious apologists either to refute Freud's theory or to achieve some kind of a compromise between psychoanalysis and religion (Beit-Hallahmi 1978). Another reaction, typically Roman Catholic, has consisted of attempts to integrate psychoanalytic concepts, but within a framework which is more descriptive than analytic (Deconchy 1967).

What makes psychoanalytic apologetics so interesting is the fact that it embraces psychoanalysis while rejecting its view of religion. What the typical psychoanalytic apologist for religion seems to say is: "Freud was right on everything, except religion." It seems rather strange that a theory is accepted as valid for the general understanding of human behavior, and then it is considered totally invalid for the understanding of a specific behavior that seems so much a part of the general theory. When a religionist rejects psychoanalysis altogether, no effort is involved and little intellectual energy is spent. The situation becomes more complex and more interesting when psychoanalysis is accepted as an essentially valid theory, except in regard to religion, and then the further step is taken of trying to prove that actually psychoanalysis supports one's religion. Everything, or almost everything psychoanalysis says is shown to be prefigured in the religious traditions involved.

GREGORY ZILBOORG: A CASE STUDY OF CHRISTIAN PSYCHOANALYTIC APOLOGETICS

Gregory Zilboorg was born in Russia of Orthodox Jewish parents in 1890, abandoned his parents' faith in his twenties, and became a member of the Society of Friends after coming to the United States at the age of twenty-nine. After becoming a psychoanalyst and a leading scholar on the history of psychiatry, he flirted with the Episcopal church, but found himself more strongly attracted to Roman Catholicism, which he officially joined in 1954, only five years before he died. In his wife's words, "Gregory died a good psychoanalyst and a good Catholic" (Zilboorg 1967, ix). Because he was a brilliant man and a serious scholar, Zilboorg's writings on psychoanalysis and religion during the last twenty years of his life constitute fascinating material for the understanding of apologetics in psychology. Zilboorg was not just an apologist for Catholicism. He was defending religion as a cultural institution against the psychoanalytic approach.

His solution to the challenge of modern psychology in general, and psychoanalysis in particular, is to maintain that the soul exists in addition to the psychic apparatus, and " . . . that what is true in psychology may not be true in traditional apologetics, Catholic, Protestant or secular, and *vice versa*—that the psychic apparatus is not the soul and the soul is not the psyche" (Zilboorg 1967, 14). So what is involved here is not only the defense of religion, but the defense of the soul. Moreover, according to Zilboorg, "Unless . . . a truly scientific differentiation between psyche and soul is made, a proper understanding and acceptance of psychoanalysis is practically impossible" (17).

As an apologist, Zilboorg takes the familiar step of discovering that there is actually no contradiction between psychoanalysis and religious tradition, and that the former actually supports the latter. This is done by reinterpreting psychoanalysis and bending it slightly. To quote Zilboorg: "Let us take as a simple example St. Thomas's assertion that sensuality is the source of evil and misuse of reason. The scientific findings of Freud demonstrated that hedonism, infantile sexuality, if persisting beyond a certain period of life leads to mental illness and other forms of a maladjustment. Here we have the scientific corroboration of the claims made by both Aristotle and St. Thomas" (36). And further:

What does matter is that Freud, unconcerned with ethics or religion, arrived at the conclusion that the life of man is based on creative love, on constant domestication of his aggression, on constant harmonization of the animal within him with his humanness, on the constant living of his life on the basis of love and reason instead of hate and impulse. The conclusions imposed themselves upon Freud by the very evidential force of the psychological phenomena which he observed clinically. It is not necessary to call upon complex philosophical speculations or to exercise much logical strain to see that Freud, unbeknown to himself, thus established an empirical basis of life which is in total conformity with the Christian ideal. (38)

And further:

One should not overlook the fact that even the concept of original sin or of the original fall of man finds its empirical counterpart in the findings of psychoanalysis. . . . Without knowing it in advance, Freud soon discovered that he was studying the psychological reactions of man in the state of sin; he was at once confronted with . . . man's perennial, unconscious sense of guilt. (45)

It may occur to us that the logic of the case may be slightly different, i.e., Freud does indeed represent and follow the accepted ideals of Western civilization of broader cultural traditions, which in turn have been influenced by Christianity.

Moreover, Zilboorg (1967) claims that Freud was unconsciously attracted to " . . . the Christian faith to which he seemed to gravitate so intensely and which he wished to deny just as intensely" (154). In all fairness, it should be recognized that Zilboorg was a brilliant scholar, and in his writings made substantive contributions not only to apologetics, but also to the psychoanalytic understanding of religion.

In Zilboorg's world view, there can be no contradiction, by definition, between religion and psychological theories or between religion and science:

Psychoanalysis itself, like physics or mathematics, permits of a number of generalizations and syntheses; but not a single one of these scientific disciplines, nor all these disciplines taken together, can be made into a philosophy of life. It is the mass of empirical data which these disciplines offer to philosophy and religion which represents their true contribution to philosophy and religion. In this respect, despite its desultory excursions into materialistic philosophy and even antireligious intellectualism, psychoanalysis has made a major contribution to the greater understanding of religious life. This again is as it should be, because no true empirical findings of facts in human nature can contradict the fundamental religious truths; what is more, the more correct and the more fundamental these facts are the more they are bound to support rather than to contradict the religious truths dealing with the destiny of man. (68)

Zilboorg quotes Pope Pius XII, in his message to Catholic psychologists (1953): "In your studies and scientific research, rest assured that no contradiction is possible between the certain truths of faith and established scientific facts. Nature, no less than revelation, proceeds from God, and God cannot contradict Himself. Do not be dismayed even if you hear the contrary affirmed insistently, even though research may have to wait for centuries to find the solution of the apparent opposition between science and faith" (277).

A typical accusation of apologists of religion against Freud is that he had selected unrepresentative samples in his study of religious phenomena. Zilboorg accuses Freud of concentrating too much on religious ritual and states that "It would appear the religion Freud had in mind was not really religion but the somewhat sentimental, somewhat anxious attitude toward God on the part of the man in the street. It is the anxious, cowering belief, of the little man, who feels the burden of what Freud calls 'the forcible imposition of mental infantilism'" (1967, 221). It seems that not only Freud but all psychologists of religion are primarily interested in "the man in the street" and his experiences, and only to a lesser extent in the experiences of some theological elite (Beit-Hallahmi 1982). "The man in the street," the "little man," represents the majority of common humanity, and the majority of common human experience. His sentimental, anxious beliefs—and not some theological abstraction—are indeed our subject matter in the psychology of religion.

JEWISH PSYCHOANALYTIC APOLOGETICS

Jewish apologetic literature is no different than any other kind of apologetics, and one sample of modern Jewish apologetics in response to and in debt to psychoanalysis is Spero's (1980) collection of essays. The treatment of psychoanalysis in this book is typical of this literature. Spero's approach to psychoanalysis is that of the apologist who desires the use of psychoanalytic theories of personality and psychoanalytic psychotherapy techniques, but rejects Freud's application of psychoanalysis to the understanding of religion.

Topics discussed by Spero in his book include "sin and neurosis," dream psychology, substance abuse, homosexuality (which is, according to the author, still both a sin and a neurosis), countertransference, contraception, and abortion. In every case, the concept or problem is discussed from the point of view of the halakha, often starting with Talmudic sources, and then studied from the point of view of psychology, mostly psychoanalysis. In many cases Spero tries to show that Talmudic insights are anticipations of later psychological notions, and in all cases an attempt is made to reconcile the two traditions. Spero attempts to show that most of the good ideas in modern psychology were already known to Talmudic sages. Such attempts are not usually very convincing. The Talmudic literature is indeed a treasury of brilliant observations on human behavior and human history, and of profound wisdom and shining wit. Still, this does not mean (as Spero seems to believe) that every modern idea has been anticipated by the Talmudic sages. Unsystematic anticipations of many modern ideas are often found in ancient writings, but these disparate anticipations are not equivalent to coherent theories. If you look hard enough, you will find anticipations of Keynesian economics, psychoanalysis, and quantum physics in ancient literature, but the ancient sages were not economists, psychologists, or physicists. Spero shares with Zilboorg the strong wish to ignore the real contradictions between religion and modern science.

4

ETHNOCENTRISM—INEVITABLE, AVOIDABLE, AND USEFUL

The psychology of religion, just like any other branch of psychology, aims at achieving generalizations and discovering the universals in human behavior. And that is why we regard religiously based differences in approaches to the psychology of religion as a problem. We are all ethnocentric to the extent that our notions of what religion is are based on a culturally skewed sample, and to the extent that our research questions and answers are determined by our cultural exposure to religion.

The influence of religious traditions may be reflected in the psychology of religion in three ways: (1) a cultural influence, which determines the way religion is defined and analyzed, and the kind of phenomena to be studied; (2) exposure to specific religious phenomena, which are then generalized and regarded as universal; and (3) religious apologetics.

One's religious tradition is going to have an effect on one's work as a psychologist of religion in terms of the choice of questions for research, the interpretation of findings, and the formulation of a general theory on religion. A specific kind of religious behavior with which the researcher is most familiar may become the model for religion in general and the basis for a general theory of religion. There is no easy way of predicting, or postdicting, a theorist's approach to religion on the basis of cultural and personal background factors. We can only attempt an analysis after the fact, taking into consideration longstanding cultural traditions, family and personality factors, and historical developments within the theorist's lifetime that affected his or her particular generation.

Psychology of Religion and Religious Background: The Case of Freud

Freud's theories are certainly the most discussed and most analyzed in the literature of the psychology of religion. In our particular context, two questions have been raised. The more general and most often raised is whether psychoanalysis in general is "Jewish" in some sense, because of Freud's cultural background. Less often mentioned is the question of whether Freud's views of religion have been formed by his own experiences with religion, in particular Judaism.

To what extent is psychoanalysis a product of, and a reflection of, Jewish culture? This question has given rise to an enormous body of literature and scholarship, with a wide range of answers (Bakan 1965; Jones 1953–57; Klein 1981; Miller 1981). Jung's comment about psychoanalysis being a "Jewish psychology" is well known and often quoted, but it has been justifiably dismissed as a bit of anti-Jewish prejudice and nothing more. Klein (1981) concludes that psychoanalysis in its beginnings under Freud was a Jewish movement, first because all the members of Freud's group in the early years were Jews, and were Jews feeling alienated and threatened because of rising anti-Semitism around them. Psychoanalysis was their way of asserting themselves against a hostile world. Freud himself had no hesitation in proclaiming and asserting a Jewish identity, though it was cultural and secular. Freud stands for a total alienation from his ancestors' religion and identity, and a complete alienation from religion as a cultural institution (Klein 1981). He represented a whole generation, or perhaps several generations, of secularized Jews. Homans (1982) suggests that Freud underwent a personal struggle against religious traditions, an active process which enabled him to create his own general theory of psychology. Such a struggle must have affected the way in which he viewed religion as an object of analysis for his theoretical system.

The question in this particular context is not the particularly "Jewish" nature of psychoanalysis, but the effects of Freud's own personal knowledge of religion in his theory. In other words, to what extent is Freud's work the result of his being exposed to particular religious traditions? Nobody can accuse Freud of being an apologist for any religion, or for religion in general. The issue in regard to Freud is whether his theory of religion is a reflection of his own familiarity with certain religious traditions. Bellah (1965) attempts to demonstrate the cultural limits of the Freudian interpretation of religious traditions.

By showing the similarities and differences between Christian and Confucian tradition in regard to father-son relations, Bellah shows the greatness and the limitations of Freud's interpretations. Freud put the theory of the projection of family relations at the center of his theory of religion. Bellah examines the Freudian model of father-son relations in religion as it holds up in the different cases of Christianity and Confucianism. His conclusion is that the Freudian model is found wanting when dealing with Chinese traditions, but this conclusion is not totally convincing. Bellah concedes that the basic Freudian idea has much merit in the understanding of Western culture, but that in China matters are more complicated. Freud's ethnocentrism (actually Europocentrism) can be easily pardoned in this case. He obviously did not have familiarity with Chinese traditions as Bellah demonstrates, but he still claimed universality for his theories. Despite obvious background limitations, it is clear that for most of the academic students of religion, Freud's theory has remained paramount.

Religious metaphors for Freud's work can be sometimes paradoxical. Thus, Zilboorg (1967) says that "Like a true Christian, Freud loved and pitied man. But also like a true Jew, he was always proud of man in a melancholy way and rather serenely anxious when he contemplated the biological strivings and limitations of man and his inordinate aggression" (21–22). Freud has known best two religious traditions: Judaism and Catholicism. Curiously enough, Freud was not only exposed to Judaism as a child, but also to Roman Catholicism. According to Jones (1953), Freud's nurse " . . . was a Catholic and used to take the young boy to attend the church services. She implanted in him the ideas of Heaven and Hell, and probably also those of salvation and resurrection. After returning from church the boy used to preach a sermon at home and expound God's doings" (6). Zilboorg (1967) suggests that when Freud discussed religion, " . . . he seems to have had foremost in his mind the Catholic Church; he lived most of his long life in Vienna and in the atmosphere of ancient Catholic traditions" (30).

The one question that has not been dealt with adequately, in my opinion, by the many scholars who have studied the relationship between Freud's Jewish background and his theory, is that of Freud's actual Jewish education. While there is no doubt that Freud was at home with Jewish folklore, he was essentially a secularized Jew, whose schooling in formal Judaism was limited. Freud's familiarity with the Old Testament as a child, attested to by many sources (Klein 1981), is not an indication of Orthodox schooling, but just its opposite. Orthodox schooling, even for children, means in Judaism the teaching of the Talmud, which is the essence of rabbinical Judaism. Thus, Freud's exposure to Judaism was that of a child in a family undergoing secularization, and he was sent to a secular state school. Nevertheless, Freud was at home with Judaism, more than with any other tradition, and it was bound to affect his conception of religion in general.

If one is mainly familiar with Judaism, a tradition with little asceticism or mysticism and with little dogma or theology, one's understanding of religion in general may become slanted. It is possible that Freud substituted Old Testament mythology for the missing dogma and theology in Judaism, and thus created the framework for the work of his followers. Freud's work on religion concentrates on the phenomena of mythology and ritual, while William James starts with the phenomena of individual mystical experiences. This might easily be seen as a reflection of the different religious phenomena Freud and James have been exposed to. It may be the peculiar nature of Judaism, as a religion of legalistic, compulsive, practices, that led Freud to his brilliant observations on the similarities between religions and individual compulsive behavior (Freud 1907).

Nevertheless, everything said so far about Freud's theory of religion in relation to his own background is only a tentative approximation. It is somewhat frustrating to admit that Freud's interpretation of religion is a personal one and cannot completely be predicted on the basis of background factors. Freud's case proves again (if such proof be needed) that it is impossible to predict the personal odyssey of a theorist, because there must be idiosyncratic causes for the selection of certain materials for analysis. The causes become less cultural and more personal when the cultural tradition is rejected, as in Freud's case.

We realize how paradoxical and how unpredictable the outcome of exposure to religious traditions may be when we look briefly at the case of a psychoanalyst who chose his own way, Erich Fromm. Fromm came from an Orthodox Jewish family, which means that he had a thorough training in Judaism, and he was a promising Talmudic scholar. His intimate knowledge of Jewish culture is evident in his writings. Later on, as a young man, he rejected Judaism completely, embracing in its place both Marxism and psychoanalysis. Given this background and this development, how can we predict Fromm's attitude toward religion? The answer is that we cannot. Despite

Fromm's rejection of Judaism and of Jewish identity, his attitude toward religion on the whole is conciliatory and even complimentary (Fromm 1950). Freud, who knew Jewish traditions more superficially, found in them and analyzed ritual and mythology. Fromm, with his strict Talmudic training, found in Judaism (and in all other religions) an ethical concern well worth preserving. His early Marxist analysis of the beginnings of Christianity (Fromm 1963), in itself a brilliant exercise, was something he neglected later on as he chose to read more and more humanistic messages in religious mythology (Fromm 1966). Fromm has become a representative of liberal Protestantism and increasingly has been associated with this movement. He came out strongly against the religious practices of his own family which, unlike Freud's, was very orthodox, but his final conception of religion was quite unique when viewed in relation to his own early experience. Ultimately, he has come to adopt a view of religion as an ethical system, completely remote from Orthodox Judaism as he had known it and much closer to liberal Protestantism. The case of Erich Fromm can be put somewhere between those of Freud and Gordon Allport, as the case of a person and a theory Americanized, or (as some would put it) sanitized and sterilized, moving from initial Marxism and psycho-analysis in their radical forms to a later version of liberal Protestantism. This particular case should provide much stimulation, and much work, for historians of ideas and for biographers.

Psychology of Religion and Religious Background: The Case of Gordon W. Allport

The psychology of religion in its American beginnings between 1880 and 1930 was the study of Protestant religious experience, with adolescent "conversion" becoming its modal behavior (Beit-Hallahmi 1974a). William James, the academic psychology of religion, and the work of Gordon W. Allport can all be regarded as growing out of the American Protestant tradition. Both James and Allport represent liberal American Protestantism in the process of becoming more individualized and more psychologized.

William James can be viewed as a representative of liberal Protestantism describing religion as a totally individual experience. James's famous definition of religion embodies this approach, which can be identified with liberal Protestantism: " . . . the feelings, acts, and experiences of individual men in their solitude, so far as they happended themselves to stand in relation to whatever they may consider the divine" (James 1961, 42). Parenthetically, I might mention that Maslow's (1964) concept of peak experiences is an idea typical of American liberal Protestantism, presented, of course, by a secularized Jewish psychologist.

Allport's *The Individual and His Religion* (1950) is a masterpiece in the William James tradition, and it deserves a place among the classics of the psychology of religion. In it Allport emphasizes that individual, subjective religious feelings are richer and livelier than institutional religion, and these unique individual experiences should be the subject matter of the psychology of religion. The kind of material that a theorist selects for analysis is the basis for his theory of religion. Freud selected mythology and the image of God the father as the subject matter for his analysis of religion. Allport, in the Jamesian tradition, selected individual, conscious experiences, in which the conscious self is the center. Against the dark and childish Freudian unconscious, which creates the myth of an omnipotent father, Allport proposes to observe the sunny mature self, confronting the world realistically and successfully

Allport can rightly be seen as the antithesis to Freud: a man at peace with his ancestors' faith, carrying on the old traditions with optimism and liberalism. To Freud's Old World pessimism, Allport is the American of Protestant positive thinking, the secure insider to Freud's "outsiderness" in regard to every tradition. Allport's attitude towards religion is best expressed in the concluding paragraph of his *chef d'oeuvre*: "A man's religion is the audacious bid he makes to bind himself to creation and the Creator. It is his ultimate attempt to enlarge and to complete his own personality by finding the supreme context in which he rightly belongs" (Allport 1950, 142).

Allport is pro-religious, but not, to use his own term (Allport and Ross 1967), "indiscriminately pro-religious." He is not in favor of every kind of religion, but only in favor of his own kind—liberal religiosity. Allport is in favor of a mature, "healthy," religion, and that is how he defines it: " . . . a disposition, built up through experience, to respond favorably, and in certain habitual ways, to conceptual objects and principles that the individual regards as of ultimate importance in his own life, and as having to do with what he regards as permanent or central in the nature of things . . ." (1950, 56). This is indeed the liberal Protestant theology of "ultimate concerns," the height of "healthy-minded" abstraction, in flight from folk religion with its mythology, and in retreat before the advance of science. This definition is indeed so abstract, and so healthy minded, that it can cover any kind of "ultimate concern," from a sports team to a political ideology. Despite its generality, which may make it useless to other theorists, this definition is important in conveying Allport's sincerity and optimism. Some of the differences between Allport and Freud can be tied to historical differences between Europe and the United States. The nature of dominant traditions and the different place of religious institutions in society lead to the gap between Freud's pessimism and Allport's (naive, to some) optimism, and to the gap between conceptions regarding the role of religion in individual and social life.

Allport came out in defense of liberal Protestantism and against conservative Protestantism in his work on religiosity and social prejudices. This whole issue, which has received so much attention in the literature since the Second World War (Allport and Kramer 1946; Allport and Ross 1967; Gorsuch and Aleshire 1974), is merely a question of the self image of liberal Protestant American psychologists when confronted with the realities of their society. But this question that grew out of ethnocentric interests and a specific cultural situation turned out to have a more general significance. According to Allport's (1966) and Freud's (1922) formulations, it may have much to do with the basic nature of religion as a group orientation. It has been studied in other places, and the same relationship has been found (Argyle and Beit-Hallahmi 1975). Thus, what started as a parochial issue has become almost a universal in the psychology of religion.

A Typology of Ethnocentrism in Social Science

The pervasive and inevitable ethnocentrism of any social science may be most in evidence when it attempts to produce a general theory, valid for all cultures, or when it examines a culture other than its own. There are four types of ethnocentric errors in the interpretation of another culture:

Type 1, in which the ethnocentric observer expresses his amazement at some phenomenon in another culture, while ignoring the existence of the same amazing elements in his own culture.

Type 2, in which the observer generalizes from his own culture to the whole of humankind.

Type 3, in which the observer creates the finding by his own idiosyncratic behavior, which in turn leads the natives to act in a special way that is then perceived as normal for the native culture.

Type 4, in which the observer misinterprets an item by not knowing its cultural context.

If there are indeed universal elements in religious behavior, then ethnocentrism is an easier problem, because students of the psychology of religion are always sampling the universal. If there are no universals in religion, then ethnocentrism is indeed a true Procrustean bed.

Bellah (1965) has given scholars a warning against ethnocentrism, together with an example of how it should be recognized and handled. Being aware of one's ethnocentric viewpoint is the beginning of wisdom. In the psychology of religion, the best antidote for inevitable ethnocentrism is an awareness of it and a willing collaboration with other scholars studying religion, in the fields of anthropology, sociology, and history. Before formulating any general notions about a psychological theory of religion, investigators should develop their "anthropological consciousness" and their historical awareness, thus keeping the psychology of religion among the human and humane sciences.

There is room and need for further research on the relationship between personal religious background of a researcher and the content of his or her research in terms of themes, formulations, questions, and answers. The study may even be limited—and this should be a useful scholarly exercise—to the various definitions of religion adopted by scholars: those definitions should be related to their authors' own experiences with religion. The examples presented above, in the cases of Freud and Allport, are just partial approximations.

Ethnocentrism, in the sense of being familiar with one religious tradition by dint of one's own cultural background, is inevitable. It should be recognized and then utilized to the advantage of psychologists as they struggle to interpret that which they are intimate with. Freud's greatness lies in his being able to do just that. Scholars engaged in the scientific study of religion are all aiming at interpreting the universals of religion, while they inevitably know only the particular and the immediate. Ethnocentrism can become an advantage as they delve deeper into what they are familiar with. Each one should openly acknowledge his or her own ethnocentrism or ethnocentrisms, and then proceed to use that familiarity as an important weapon in his arsenal. Being thoroughly familiar with one religious tradition is a source of strength if it enables the investigator to capture its essence. If indeed there are universal elements in religious traditions, then they should be in evidence in all traditions. Being an expert on one religion thus becomes a source of potential universalism, rather than a hindrance, as long as one is cautious in generalizing from specifics. Looking for the general in the particular rather than generalizing from particulars should be the preferred method.

5

THE STUDY OF RELIGION AND ACADEMIC PSYCHOLOGY

To say that psychologists have neglected religion as an object of study would be patently wrong, but finding traces of all the work done by psychologists in this area would be difficult, and most contemporary academic psychologists would be hard pressed to say anything if invited to give a five minute talk on "The Psychology of Religion." References to religion would be found in the writings of many major psychologists, if they were diligently searched for, but systematic treatments of the subject are rare. Among the "psychologies of. . . ," the psychology of religion is in a respectable place in terms of the number of books and articles devoted to it; more problematic is the quality of the work and its relationship to other developments in psychology. While many books on the psychology of religion can be found on library shelves, references to religion or to the psychological study of religion are rare in psychology textbooks. One way of measuring the impact and importance of the psychology of religion today is by looking at the treatment given to it in introductory psychology texts. Such texts aim to reflect the state of knowledge and activity in the field as a whole; this is their survey function. They also perform an important gatekeeping function, since they present an authoritative view of the field to the newcomer and are likely to channel his budding interests. Most introductory textbooks in psychology ignore religion completely, while some mention it once or twice. Courses on the psychology of religion are offered only rarely in academic departments of psychology. They are more likely to be taught in divinity schools, theological seminaries, or religion departments.

Social psychology seems to be the natural subfield of psychology which should be studying religion, because religion lends itself easily to analysis in social psychological terms, such as beliefs, attitudes, values, and norms. Social psychologists, with a few commendable exceptions (Bem 1970; Festinger et al. 1956; Rokeach 1968), have not used religious beliefs as the subject matter for their research and theorizing on beliefs and attitudes. Among the notable exceptions, Bem (1970) presents a lively and penetrating discussion of religious beliefs in a textbook that deals with beliefs and actions "in the real world." Fishbein and Ajzen (1974) use religious activities to test the question of the relationship between attitudes and behavior, and theirs is probably the only study of its kind. The general flight into the laboratory in social psychology and the trend away from natural social behavior included religion as well. Most social psychology textbooks simply do not mention religion under any name, shape, or form. Searching for the term "religion" in the index of standard psychology textbooks, be they in general psychology, social psychology, or personality theory, will be fruitless in most cases. Going beyond the textbooks and into a perusal of the major academic journals, where psychology is being "made," our search for articles dealing with religion will be similarly fruitless. The typical academic journal in psychology will deal with religious materials only rarely. This is another form of "canonization," because the journals determine the boundaries of legitimate work, and it is a reflection of the limited research on religious phenomena done in academic psychology. That the psychological study of religion is of interest to only a small minority in psychology has been reported by Malony (1972). He found, in a random sample of APA members, that only 1.1% reported an interest in studying religion.

Despite the significant historical contributions to the study of religion, the area has not been integrated into mainline academic psychology. If inclusion in introductory textbooks is the academic equivalent of scriptural canonization, it is clear that the study of religion has remained outside the canon of academic psychology. The reasons for this exclusion will be discussed in the following sections.

The Reluctance to Approach Religion as a Subject of Study

Paradoxical and contradictory forces have shaped the attitudes of psychologists toward the study of religion. Hostility to religion, support for religion, and fear of religion all combine to hamper scholarly work. There may be two loci of resistance—within psychology and within the culture. In all social sciences there may be traces of the cultural taboo against a close study of religion from a scholarly viewpoint. Religion, both as a social institution in the abstract and as concrete social institutions and individuals, defends itself against close scrutiny. Psychologists may be concerned about stepping on too many cultural toes, which may result from studying religion. Religious beliefs still enjoy a tabooed status in Western society, and the religious establishment is not totally powerless. The longstanding cultural taboo against looking at religion too closely is still affecting scholars in the age of secularization. Glock and Stark (1965) refer to the resistance on the part of religious organizations as a problem in studies of religion by the social sciences.

Empirical research in behavioral sciences does not exist in a social vacuum. It is supported or hindered by its social environment. Part of this environment is the academic community itself, but sources of pressure extend far beyond the universities. Most psychological research projects have been supported by outside sources, especially by the United States government. Applicants for research grants have to defend the importance and relevance of the projects, and it is doubtful whether many psychologists have proposed projects dealing with religious behavior. From the government's side, it is also doubtful whether much encouragement would have been given those who had applied. Discussions during the uproar in 1965 over invasion of privacy in psychological testing made it clear that members of the United States Congress considered questions on religion in psychological research undesirable (Gallagher 1966). These discussions also made it clear that government support would not be forthcoming for any research dealing specifically with questions of religious beliefs, beyond those concerned with nominal religious affiliation.

Though it may seem logical that religious organizations would be a natural source of support for psychologists interested in studying religion, only limited work has been sponsored by these. The attitude of religious organizations to research on religious behavior is ambivalent. Glock and Stark (1965) have suggested that any serious systematic study of religion which follows the canons of social science must be a threat to religious institutions. Leuba (1916) wrote about the resistance to scientific studies of religious beliefs: "It is rather the old desire to protect 'Holy things' from too close scrutiny, and also the more or less unconscious antagonism of those interested in the maintenance of the status quo in religion that have stood in the way of those who might have been disposed to face the difficulties of a statistical investigation of religious convictions" (175).

The Study of Religion and the "Paradigm" of Academic Psychology

The psychological study of religion is outside the mainstream of academic psychology because it does not fit into the dominant model in the field. If we follow James's division between the tough minded and the tender minded (1907), it is easy to see why psychology's approach to religion will be that of rejection and distance. Modern psychology is undoubtedly tough minded, and thus it will be empiricist, materialistic, skeptical, and irreligious. Several biases in academic psychology work against the study of religion. Psychology today can be said to be mostly ahistorical, acultural, and anti-introspective. Psychologists prefer to study general psychological processes, rather than the specific content of these processes; thus, psychologists study memory as process, regardless of the specific material remembered. A case may be made for the claim that there is nothing unique about religion in terms of psychological processes. Instead, what defines religion is a specific content that is rather relative, historical, and constantly changing. Because psychologists pursue a theoretical ideal of studying ahistorical, universal mental processes, and not mental content; religion falls outside the field of subjects deemed appropriate for study.

The triumph of positivism and operationalism contributed to the desire to stay away from religion, on pain of contamination by "unscientific" attitudes. Religion reminds psychology of its "unscientific" past, with ideas of the soul, absolute judgments, and untestable beliefs. Some psychologists may wish that this embarrassing relic would disappear, since they believe that what they are engaged in signifies a triumph over the old, mistaken traditions. The academic study of religion in general may be perceived as a threat to " . . . science, reason, logic, and the whole heritage of the Enlightenment" (Bellah 1970, 113). This perception may be exaggerated, but it is not always completely without foundation. In the case of psychology, as we shall see, it is true that those who study religion are also promoting it, so that the reaction to the study of religion is a reaction to religion itself.

The subject of religion seems too complex and too soft for the laboratory paradigm. It is filled with much imagination and feelings, two topics which academic psychology finds hard to approach. The dominant methodology in academic psychology has been that of experimentation, most of the time on nonhuman animals. While it is obvious that experiments on the religious practices of white rats are hard to conduct, experimental studies of religion in humans are also frought with ethical and practical problems. Some "experimental" or "quasi-experimental" work has been done in the psychology of religion, using the dominant laboratory model in psychology (Osarchuk and Tate 1973; Deconchy 1977).

It is unclear whether experimentation in the psychology of religion would have been very fruitful (cf. Batson 1977; Deconchy 1985), but it is certain that the lack of experimentation has contributed to the alienation of the field from mainstream psychology. The issue is not only of the limitations on experiments but also of the uselessness of animal models, which have been popular in most areas of psychology. The relative neglect of religion as a subject matter in psychology is not terribly different from the relative neglect of other cultural, "soft" areas. If the ideal and the dominant paradigm is that of the laboratory, it is not surprising that the subject matter of art, literature, and religion will be relegated to the dusty corners of psychology libraries. The "humanistic" criticism of mainstream psychology (Hudson 1972) seems fully justified in this case: academic psychology seems to run away from meaningful human behavior. The scant attention paid by academic psychology to religion would be included by critics of academic psychology among the indications of its irrelevance to most significant human bahaviors. It is possible to generalize and say that academic psychologists stay away from products of the human imagination, either individual or cultural.

Secularization and the Study of Religious Behavior

There can be little doubt that the decline in the interest that psychologists have shown in religion as an area of study parallels the decline in the importance of religion as a social institution. The latter decline is a major fact of modern history and modern society (Wilson 1966; Argyle and Beit-Hallahmi 1975). In a private conversation with a colleague a few years ago, I heard the following statement: "I am not interested in religion, because religion doesn't make a difference in the lives of individuals anyway." This strong claim can find some support in the research literature, and it may justify the neglectful attitude on the part of psychologists. Religion is gradually disappearing from the face of the earth, and even when it exists it exerts in most cases only little influence. This argument against studying religion does have some validity, especially in connection with individual dynamics. Religiosity and religious affiliation are found to be correlated with sociological variables (i.e., group traits) rather than with psychological variables (i.e., individual traits). In a secularized world, religion may be seen as a social label, helpful in predicting some group trends, but of minor significance in explaining individual motivation. However, despite the evidence for secularization, there are indications that the religious subidentity will remain significant because of specific features of modern society (Wilson 1966).

6

ACADEMIC PSYCHOLOGY STUDIES RELIGION: FINDINGS, GENERALIZATIONS, AND THEORETICAL QUESTIONS

This section will briefly review what in the language of academic psychology are known as "findings," i.e., results of conventional psychological research that according to established criteria are admissible into the court of social science. Included here are findings that are beyond dispute and are supported by numerous studies; more detailed reports summarizing the research literature are found in Dittes (1969) and Argyle and Beit-Hallahmi (1975). These findings all belong to what is customarily called the social psychology of religion, i.e., the effort to find behavior and social background correlates of religiosity and religious affiliation. They provide answers to some interesting questions about religion, but they are often the results of atheoretical research. Some of the findings give partial answers to some of the "classical questions" in the psychological study of religion, and we will turn first to those. Later on, we will present some theoretical issues which point to both problems and possibilities.

The Consequences of Religiosity

Glock (1962), in one of the best known and most frequently used formulations in social science literature on religion, proposed the following five dimensions of religiosity:

1. ideological, covering religious beliefs
2. intellectual, covering religious knowledge
3. ritualistic, covering participation in religious rituals

4. experiential, covering intense religious experiences
5. consequential, covering the consequences of religiosity in non-religious activities

Dittes (1969), following Glock (1962), lists the category of *religious effects* among five categories of religious variables in psychological research. Religious effects were defined as "implications of religion for 'conduct' in 'secular' affairs" (609). These include "experience of immediate rewards: for example, peace of mind, freedom from worry . . ., obedience to concrete and specific prescriptions . . ., [and] applications of general principles" (609).

Discovering such consequences has not been easy, and later on, as the result of further research, the consequential dimension was dropped; the reason was given that such consequences in nonreligious behavior could not be found, and only four dimensions have remained (Glock and Stark 1966). These four dimensions are widely used. One problem in the study of consequences is logical and methodological. Most of the research done on consequences is correlational; it cannot indicate causality. Even when more detailed comparisons are made between groups, the question of screening out nonreligious variables remains. It is always safer to assume that secular factors lead to secular behaviors, but traditionally religion is tied to the expectation of consequences in the secular sphere. The main reason for the expectation of consequences is that religious traditions quite explicitly predict those consequences. Religion exists for many believers as a prescriptive behavior system, containing specific shoulds and shouldn'ts; for other believers, however, religion is a proscriptive rather than prescriptive system, and from the psychological viewpoint is concerned mainly with impulse control. The findings (Argyle and Beit-Hallahmi 1975) show that religion does have a considerable effect on secular behavior in two areas: sexual behavior and the use of drugs. In these two areas, specific religious prohibitions seem to have a considerable effect in controlling individual behavior. But these effects exist only where a specific proscription exists. Generalizing beyond these specific areas has been difficult.

The expectation that religiosity would lead to some kind of general social attitude in response to the traditional moral exhortations of religious representatives has not been supported by the research. Religious people are not more likely to engage in positive social actions, be more honest, or be more generous (Argyle and Beit-Hallahmi 1975). The well-known findings about the positive correlation between religiosity and prejudice have been mentioned in this context, but it is hard to view them as specific consequences of religiosity. The best explanation for the correlation between religiosity and prejudice, authoritarianism, and conservatism may be sociological rather than psychological. Religious people are most likely to be conservative in their general world view, and they tend to support the traditional beliefs of their cultures in nonreligious areas. The question of consequence is related to the question of the religious personality, which is the search for consequences on an individual personality level.

THE SEARCH FOR THE "RELIGIOUS PERSONALITY"

When investigators search for the sources of religious motivation, a distinction is often being made between genuine religious motives and secondary or external motives. This problematic distinction has been addressed by Allport and Ross (1967) and others through the suggested intrinsic-extrinsic dimension of religious belief. Actually, this is the old tradition of differentiating between the "true believer" who puts his heart and soul into his faith (or his faith into his heart and soul) and the follower of religion who pays only lip service to its tenets because of external considerations. These two psychological types may be defined through other personality traits. But the attractive distinction between the "true believers" and the conventionally religious has been bogged down in the mire of empirical measurements. The dimension proposed by Allport and Ross (1967) has been found to be lacking in validity and consistency (cf. Meadow and Kahoe 1984). One finding is clear, and that is that the majority of churchgoers belong to the extrinsic category, the "true" believers having always been, and having remained in the minority.

Something which the layman expects of the psychologist dealing with religion is a psychological description of the religious person. The layman may ask, with some justification, what the religious person is like and how he is different from the nonreligious person. Religion expects the religious person to be different and tells him to be different. So one natural task, and maybe a most natural one, of the psychology of religion is to describe the psychological profile of the religious person. The obstacles to the completion of this task have been many. Numerous studies have tried to contribute to the hoped for psychological profile (see Beit-Hallahmi 1973b; Brown 1973; Paloutzian 1983), but the results have been disappointing so far. The first obstacle, as we have seen above, is that of defining the truly religious person. What we are able to conclude about the religious person in Western society today is that he is probably more conventional, authoritarian, dogmatic, and suggestible than the nonreligious person. Dittes (1969) reflects another judgment when he states that ". . . psychological research reflects an overwhelming consensus that religion (at least as measured in the research, usually institutional affiliation or adherence to conservative traditional doctrines) is associated with awareness of personal inadequacies, either generally or in response to particular crisis or threat situations; with objective evidence of inadequacy, such as low intelligence; with a strong responsiveness to the suggestions of other persons or other external influences; and with an array of what may be called desperate and generally unadaptive defense measures" (616).

Why have the attempts to relate personality variables and religiosity been unsuccessful? One reason is the complexity of variables and measurements that researchers are dealing with. The field of personality research in recent years has been in a state of upheaval. The most extreme position suggested was that we no longer need to look for stable oversituational personality traits, since they do not exist anyway. Less extreme positions have emphasized the idea of the interaction, i.e., that behavior is a function of both stable traits from the inside and presses of the situation from outside, and those traits, needs, and presses all change over time. Sounds complicated? Well, it is. When psychologists try to involve this complexity in studying religious behavior, which is in itself complex and overdetermined, it is small wonder that they do not arrive at any easy generalizations. Another reason why relating personality variables and religious behavior has been less than successful is historical. What secularization means on the psychological level is that there is less detectable influence of religion on individual personality and behavior.

One may ask the question, "Does religion, in our secularized society, make a difference in anybody's life?" This question has been asked by Bouma (1970), and his answer was that indeed we are able to prove only a marginal influence of religion in any area of modern life. Religion nevertheless may remain useful for predicting group trends and may serve as a significant identity label.

Social-Psychological Findings

The following findings are summarized from Argyle and Beit-Hallahmi (1975) and Paloutzian (1983):

1. Religious behavior is obviously culturally and socially conditioned. This may sound like a truism, but it is an important and elementary truth that tends to be neglected quite often. Social learning, despite its seeming simplicity (and maybe because of it), remains the best explanation for most religious actions. Actually, as we look closer at more unusual and "esoteric" religious actions is becomes clear that they are socially learned, just like the less esoteric ones. To the question, "Why do people believe in God?" the best answer remains: "Because they have been taught to believe in God." The variety of religious traditions and the correspondence between the tradition of the social environment and the religious beliefs of the individual are the most obvious proofs to the validity of the social learning approach, which is also able to explain what are considered intense religious experiences (Spanos and Hewitt 1979).

2. In accordance with *1*, above, the effects of parental beliefs are more important than any other factor in determining individual religiosity.

3. Unmarried individuals are likely to be more involved in religious activities than married individuals.

4. Adolescence is the period of religious "conversions" that are experiences of personal recommitment to a familiar religious tradition. These differ from true conversions, which involve the change from religious tradition *A* to religious tradition *B*, such as the cases of Thomas Merton (Merton 1948) and Alphonse Ratisbone (James 1902).

5. There is a decline in religious involvement during the third decade of life.

6. There is a rise in religious involvement after age thirty that continues into old age.

7. Women are higher than men on every measure of religiosity and religious involvement. They are also more likely to support para-religious, parapsychological, and pseudoscientific beliefs (e.g., Markle, Peterson, and Wagenfeld, 1978).

8. There is a slight negative correlation between religiosity and I.Q.

9. Religiosity is correlated with the traits of authoritarianism, dogmatism, and suggestibility.
10. Religiosity is positively correlated with ethnocentrism and political conservatism.
11. Religiosity does not affect suicidal behaviors.
12. Religiosity is negatively correlated with sexual activity, as measured by "total sexual outlet."
13. Religiosity is positively correlated with better adjustment in marriage and lower frequency of divorce.

THE HISTORICITY OF FINDINGS IN THE STUDY OF RELIGION

An important realization in regard to research in the social psychology of religion is that the answers to the questions that this field attempts to cover are often historical in nature. This argument has been raised in connection with other areas of psychological research. Psychologists are supposed to be looking for universal laws and generalizations, and they believe that this search is feasible in principle and hampered in practice only by technical difficulties. However, it is possible that the search may be more difficult than hitherto expected. A source of doubt and criticism among psychologists over the past few years has been the growing realization of the timebound nature of psychological findings. Psychologists have realized that the more general questions in social psychology and in personality research have answers that are always tied to specific historical situations. The historicity of psychological findings is being noted more and more often. Atkinson (1974) suggested that any empirical relationship between personality variables describes only a "modal personality" at a particular historical moment.

Gergen (1973) claimed that ". . . social psychological research is primarily the systematic study of contemporary history. As such, it seems myopic to maintain disciplinary detachment from (a) the traditional study of history, and (b) other historically bound sciences (including sociology, political science and economics)" (319). Furthermore, Gergen (1973) stated that ". . . social psychology is primarily an historical enquiry. Unlike the natural sciences, it deals with facts that are largely nonrepeatable and which fluctuate markedly over time. . . . Knowledge cannot accumulate in the usual scientific sense because such knowledge does not generally transcend its historical boundaries" (310). Theories of social behavior turn out to be reflections of contemporary history, and the business of psychology, just like the business of history, is never finished. The strong reaction to Gergen's arguments shows how much psychology is attached to a certain conception of its own nature as a science, a notion which is based on ideas taken from the natural sciences.

The notion of the transhistorical and transcultural nature of certain behaviors is especially prevalent in the study of religion. Religious beliefs and religious sentiments seem to have been in existence everywhere in every historical period. Telling the cultural and temporal from the transcultural and transhistorical may be one aim of the psychology of religion. Cultural differences in space, of which we are already aware, may be equaled by historical differences, of which we are now becoming increasingly conscious. The historicity of findings regarding the social psychology of religion is evident in any survey of such findings (Argyle and Beit-Hallahmi 1975). It becomes clear that the psychological impact of religion in modern societies is changing and becoming more limited as a result of secularization. Psychologists of religion, while describing contemporary situations, are mainly writing the chronicles of secularization. One conclusion they are able to reach nevertheless is that the impact of religion is differential. There are certain areas of behavior, such as sexual activity, where religion has a clear influence, while in most other areas the impact of religion is limited. There may be different kinds of psychological motives for private and public religious acts. In the context of secularization, private religious acts may be the more "psychological" ones, while public religious acts may be explained on purely social grounds.

QUESTIONS FOR FUTURE WORK

It seems that the surface has barely been scratched; many interesting questions can be asked in regard to the psychological aspect of religion as a living institution. It seems that the classical question in the psychological study of religion has been phrased as follows: "Does religion, or religiosity, make a difference in individual behavior and individual personality?" This question of consequences in behavior and personality has been the most common other than the question of the psychological nature of religion itself. The reason for the emphasis on consequences has been historical and cultural. Historically, religion has been thought of and described as a "moral system," concerned with the morality or immorality of specific behaviors and with the definition of transgression and sin. The traditional view of religion as a prescriptive-proscriptive system whose aim is to create a difference in individual behavior has led to the expectation of differences in actual behavior. This expectation may have to be changed.

Historically, the influence of religion is diminishing. Religion will make less of a difference in individual behavior as the worldwide process of secularization continues. Moreover, there are many human activities that are engaged in for themselves, without any additional consequences expected. Such activities are commonly referred to as art or entertainment. Psychologists do not expect any effects in subsequent behavior when people go to museums, theaters, or athletic events; why should they expect any effects when they go to church? (See the discussion in Chapter 8 on "Religion as Art".) In light of this, it is possible that they have been looking for the wrong kind of consequence, using the wrong kind of instruments.

One of the functions of religion, according to "cognitive need" theories in the social sciences, is to supply both individuals and societies with a meaning system for life events. If religion is indeed a personal meaning system, the questions to be answered are when and how often religious explanations are used for personal or nonpersonal events. If religion is a meaning system and a system of moral guidance, designed to affect individual moral decisions, how does this process take place in reality? How often do individuals ascribe religious meanings to events in their everyday life? How often is religion taken into consideration in moral decisions? Despite the fact that these concerns are a major part of religious traditions, psychology still knows very litle about them. It is plausible to assume that religious belief systems are not used often or are used only as a last resort in modern society. If religion is indeed an individual or a social meaning system, then it is quite clear that its function as a meaning system is quite limited; it does not ever include every sphere of human experience. Even in the most religious culture there are always certain objects or occasions which are outside the realm of holiness. Otherwise, how would holiness be defined? Cultures may differ quantitatively, of course, in the extent to which religious meaning is given to human experiences, and this may be a psychological index of secularization. What can be said is that for most humans today the religious meaning system, if extant at all, is well circumscribed and rather narrow. The boundaries of the religious meaning system should be an intriguing question for psychological research.

7
PSYCHOANALYSIS AND THE PSYCHOLOGICAL STUDY OF RELIGION

Dynamic psychology in general and psychoanalysis in particular have had more to say about religious actions than have the various movements in conventional academic psychology. Psychoanalysis is the one psychological approach to the understanding of religion which has had a major effect both on religion as an institution and on the study of religion in all human sciences. Psychoanalytic approaches to the question of culture and religion, and to the question of individual integration in society, have affected all social science disciplines (e.g., Kardiner and Linton 1945; Parsons 1951, 1960). The psychoanalytic study of religious beliefs and institutions has drawn considerable attention on the part of scholars in the fields of religion, history, sociology, and anthropology. The psychoanalytic psychology of religion can be divided into two main parts: the original writings of Freud himself (see Pruyser 1973, and Beit-Hallahmi 1978), and further contributions by his students and followers, such as those by Rank (1914), Reik (1946, 1951), Jones (1951), and Erikson (1958, 1966). The best articulated contemporary presentation of the psychoanalytic approach to religion is that by La Barre (1972), which combines Freudian theory with a rich collection of cultural and historical case studies.

The Psychoanalytic Psychology of Religion

Psychoanalysis is the only major psychological theory which offers an explanation of religion as part of a comprehensive theory of human behavior. Religion is presented as an instance of general psychological forces in action (cf. Dittes 1969). Freud's theoretical explanation for the origin and existence of religion is based on certain presumed universal psychological experiences and processes: the experience of helplessness, the tendency for compensation through fantasy, and the experience of early relations with protective figures. Every individual is psychologically prepared by these universal experiences to accept religious ideas that are obviously culturally transmitted. The question about the world of spirits is: does this world exist "out there," and if it does not, where is it? The psychological answer given by psychoanalysis, is that it exists within, in our own mental apparatus and our own mental abilities to fantasize and project. The world of spirits, the supernatural world unseen and somehow felt in religious experience, is a projection of the internal world. Psychoanalytic theory explains both the origin of the supernatural premise and its specific contents.

An eloquent summary of the psychoanalytic explanation for the world of the spirits has been offered by Muensterberger (1972): "Who are the gods who panic? Who are the monsters and werewolves, ogres and witches? Or the bogeys, vampires, and vultures who appear in dreams and mysteries and threaten one's life? Whence those fears and figments; the notion of fantastic beings and domains no human is able to fathom? We encounter them everywhere. They are an integral part of the vast repertoire of human imagination, nay, the human condition. Their supernatural craft stems from that inspiration which is one way or the other belongs inevitably to everyone's childlike sense of impending doom or disaster and only magic, ritual, or prayer can tame or dispel" (ix).

Paradoxically, psychoanalysis is less individualistic in its biases, and this becomes clear when we look at the materials that have been used in psychoanalytic interpretations of religion (Beit-Hallahmi 1978), which have consisted mostly of mythology, socially transmitted materials which the individual responds to. Freud's theory does not suggest that the individual creates his religion *de novo* as he grows up, but that childhood experiences within the family prepare the individual for the cultural system of religion. Psychoanalysis sees every religious act, every religious belief or ritual, as the appropriate unit of analysis. There is no need for special sampling, since every unit of behavior is equally representative. The same basic method can be used to analyze a whole mythical system or one individual believer. The psychoanalytic paradigm enables us to analyze both process and content in religion (cf. Pruyser 1973).

Freud's contributions are to date the most ambitious attempt to present a comprehensive nonreligious interpretation of religion in Western culture and history. The topics Freud dealt with include, first of all, a developmental theory of religion, both phylogenetically and ontogenetically. Freud also attempted to explain the functions and consequences of religion for both society and the individual. In this area, as in many others, Freud's writings offer a rich variety of hypotheses regarding various religious beliefs and practices.

Some of the better-known hypotheses derived from psychoanalytic theory are the father-projection hypotheses (Argyle and Beit-Hallahmi 1975), the superego projection hypothesis (Argyle and Beit-Hallahmi 1975), and the obsessional neurosis hypothesis. These hypotheses can be interpreted both phylogenetically and ontogenetically. Among Freud's followers, Theodor Reik and Ernest Jones are those who followed him most closely, creating in effect essays in "applied psychoanalysis" by applying Freud's principles of interpretation to specific religious acts. Many other, less known exercises in psychoanalytic interpretation are scattered in various journals (Beit-Hallahmi 1978).

Quantitatively, psychoanalysis has contributed more to the psychology of religion than any other theoretical approach. More publications dealing with all aspects of religion can be identified with the psychoanalytic approach than with any other school or orientation. At the same time, the actual impact of the psychoanalytic approach is much more limited than could be expected on the basis of quantity alone. The major qualitative characteristics of psychoanalytic interpretations of religion is that they deal more often with the substance of religious beliefs and myths and less often with function and structure.

The literature of psychoanalysis following Freud has concentrated on religious mythology and ritual rather than on religious experiences as its subject matter. A quantitative analysis of psychoanalytic writings shows that mythology is a major topic, while religious experience receives less attention than it gets from other theoretical approaches. Out of about four hundred psychoanalytic studies dealing with religion along classical lines, less than ten percent have for a topic individual religious experiences. About fifty percent deal with mythology, and the rest deal with dogma and ritual (see Beit-Hallahmi 1978).

Methodologically, most psychoanalytic publications studying religious phenomena can be characterized by their structure and style. We can use the term "a modal article," identified by several common characteristics. These include the choice of a myth or belief to be discussed, rather than individual experience, and the use of material taken from anthropology, comparative religion, or archaeology. Often, clinical material is introduced after the analysis of historical material to show parallels between individual and cultural processes. The model for this way of analysis is the clinical analysis of a dream or a symptom. The religious belief or behavior is selected as the segment of human action to be analyzed in order to discover an unconscious (or at least unknown to the involved person) meaning. The assumption is that religious acts are always psychologically meaningful, and that the same rules apply to the analysis of individual and cultural products. The psychoanalytic style of studying religion becomes, then, very similar to the style of clinical discussion.

Assessing the effects of the psychoanalytic approach on the psychology of religion in general involves considering facts both inside and outside of the psychoanalytic movement. There is a general impression that the influence of psychoanalysis is waning and that there is decline in the number of psychoanalytic studies of religion. While it is clear that psychoanalysis does have a reduced role in the psychology of religion, psychoanalytic studies of religion have not disappeared from the intellectual scene. They have become more esoteric, because they are usually published in psychoanalytic journals and are not usually read by the uninitiated. Their sphere of influence is thus limited.

Object relations theory, the most important theoretical development in psychoanalysis since Freud (Guntrip 1968; Winnicott 1971), provides the best theoretical basis for understanding the world of spirits in relation to the internal world of objects. Rubenstein (1963) complained about the research lag in psychoanalytic studies of religion, which were still using the old instinctual framework while the newer object relations framework was already available. This gap is beginning to be closed now (e.g., Rizzuto 1979), and future work based on this approach promises to illuminate religion in all its varied manifestations.

One indication of the importance of the psychoanalytic interpretation of religion is the reaction to it on the part of religionists and religious institutions. Psychoanalysis has been the major psychological challenge to Western religion in the twentieth century. For religionists, psychoanalysis has remained a problem, as indicated by the number of books and articles written from a religious viewpoint and attempting to respond to that challenge. "If the status of depth psychology as insider or outsider has provoked the dialogue between theology and psychology, we must note that the archoutsider (or -insider), Freud himself, continues to make himself felt whenever religion and theology take psychology seriously" (Homans 1968b, 8).

Criticism of the psychoanalytic approach to religion has been voiced often, not only by religionists but also by sympathetic social scientists. One of the common complaints is the psychoanalytic tendency to overinterpret and overpsychologize, while neglecting the historical and cultural components of the phenomena under analysis. Of course, such accusations of "psychological imperialism" are made against psychological approaches in general from the perspective of other disciplines, and the avoidance of such imperialism should be a basic methodological concern to all psychologists. Another kind of criticism, which is specific to psychoanalysis, is that it uses a model of psychopathology to explain the phenomena of religion, either as a substantive approach (phenomenon X is the expression of psychopathology, be it a "trance" state or a certain religious persuasion) or an analogy (the dynamics of religious actions are identical to those of psychopathological symptoms—religion as a universal compulsive neurosis). To this criticism there are several answers. First, a dynamic approach to psychopathology means that underlying processes and forces are looked for, and they may be the same for pathological and nonpathological behavior. Second, there is a great deal of interaction between certain religious experiences and psychopathology, as clinical data indicate (e.g., Cavenar and Spaulding 1977). Third, there may be more psychopathology in individuals and cultures than they are ready to admit. The Freudian emphasis on pathology teaches us some humility. Being neurotic is not the exception; it is the rule. And so, the use of psychopathology as a model may be more appropriate than we are ready to admit in our natural narcissism.

Within psychoanalysis itself, new theoretical developments have taken the place of the emphasis on Oedipal and instinctual motives that had been typical of the psychoanalytic study of religion. The rise of object relations theory and the attention given pre-Oedipal experiences have broadened the scope of the basic psychoanalytic view of personal and cultural phenomena. As a result, many psychoanalytic studies seem obsolete or narrow in their approach. Another common source of criticism is the use psychoanalysts make of historical and archaeological findings. There is little doubt that psychoanalytic works can be criticized on scholarly grounds, and that psychoanalysts may be poor scholars either in the application of their own theory or in their borrowing from other fields. Still, the weaknesses of specific applications may not negate the value of the general approach.

On the positive side, the psychoanalytic mode of analysis may be adopted as a general mode for viewing religion in the context of culture, with more attention given to social and cultural factors. The impressive body of work inspired by psychoanalysis cannot be dismissed or ignored by the contemporary psychology of religion. The relative neglect demonstrated by psychologists of religion toward psychoanalysis may turn into positive interest when its contribution is viewed in perspective and the usual scholarly criteria is applied to it.

8

FIRST ATTEMPT AT A THEORY: RELIGION AS ART

The most common theme in the literature on the psychology of religion is the search for psychological processes unique to religion (see Dittes 1969). I would like to present here a contrasting viewpoint, which states that religion is not unique in terms of process, but rather in terms of content. The psychological processes involved in religious activities can be found in other human activities. Art is one example of human activity in which processes similar to those operating in religion are involved, and through looking at the psychology of art, investigators may gain useful insights into the psychology of religion.

This may be not just a useful way, but a major way of understanding religion, because religion, like art, is so readily recognized for being an expressive, noninstrumental, and pervasive human activity. At the least, this would be a useful intellectual exercise, providing insights through the application of analogies. At the most, it would be a way of obtaining major new insights into religion. Art is simply the most similar to religion among all spheres of human activity, and that is why I propose using it as a starting point. Art is used here as a general category, denoting a wide range of human activity, and religion as a more limited case, exemplifying the basic processes of the general category of art.

Presenting an analogy, or finding an analogy for something one is studying, is a way of gaining new understandings and insights. Scientific creativity consists of finding fruitful analogies and metaphors, normally referred to as models. Here I am suggesting a metaphor and a model that will contribute to the development of a general theory of religion. The starting point, the moment of discovery, can be summarized as a metaphor in the sense adopted by Black (1962): "Metaphor is, at its simplest, a way of proceeding from the known to the unknown. It is a way of cognition in which the identifying qualities of one thing are transferred in an instantaneous, almost unconscious, flash of insight to some other thing that is, by remoteness, or complexity, unknown to us. . . . Metaphor is our means of effecting instantaneous fusion of two separated realms of experience into one illuminating, iconic, encapsulating image" (4). Pepper (1942) has used the term "root metaphor," or basic analogy, which he explains as follows:

> The method in principle seems to be this: A man desiring to understand the world looks about for a clue to its comprehension. He pitches upon some area of common-sense fact and tries if he cannot understand other areas in terms of this one. The original area then becomes his *basic analogy* or *root metaphor*. . . .
>
> A list of its structural characteristics becomes his basic concepts of explanation and description. We call them a set of categories. . . . In terms of these categories he proceeds to study all other areas of fact whether uncriticized or previously criticized. He undertakes to interpret all facts in terms of these categories. (91)

This analogy between art and religion is based on the belief that both can be explained with the help of basic and common psychological processes. The ideas expressed here are only a preliminary contribution, but the main point is intended to be taken quite seriously: looking at religion as a form of art may be a considerable advance over previous attempts to develop a coherent psychology of religion. Using art as a starting point in formulating observations may help in understanding the basic process, the functions, and the consequences of religion.

The problem in defining and describing religion are quite similar to the problems of defining and describing art, and disagreements on the results abound. There are also disagreements on the function of both in society. In everyday discussions, there is often disagreement on the difinition of art, since the criteria used, both implicit and explicit, are evaluative (i.e., art has to be "good"). When it comes to a psychological definition, I propose to use the criterion of reaction: art resides in objects which are designed to create an emotional reaction in the observer (reader, listener) without satisfying any other (more basic) needs. This criterion of reaction is relevant to both art and religion.

Art is often viewed as the opposite of real life, as an opposite of practicality and instrumentality, and indeed it is noninstrumental, but at the same time it is vital to human existence. Langer (1953) has put religion together with art in the same category of nondiscursive human activities.

In modern society, both art and religion are sheltered deviations—protected from the so-called rationality of the marketplace and from the real rationalization of the production process. The image of the artist in this society is similar to the image of the religious person. They are both "soft" deviants, emotional and feminine. Both religion and art, in a certain common frame of reference, are seen as impractical and irrelevant to many important social and human concerns. Art is most often conceived as something with no practical relevance to many pressing issues, and religion likewise is considered "spiritual," which often means uncontaminated by real issues, especially political ones. To summarize the basic psychological similarities between the institution of art and the institution of religion in human society, one might say that both institutions are expressive, i.e., noninstrumental, emotional, irrational, and "feminine."

Religion, like art, is a form and a product of human labor. It is a system created by humans and a proof of human activity and genius. To put this claim in the strongest possible terms: religion is a work of art. It is (for believers and even for nonbelievers) beautiful, harmonious, pleasing, and attractive. In a confused, confusing, and cruel world, where mankind feels helpless before nature and history, religion and art provide order and beauty. Religion and art are both comforting illusions in a world which makes such illusions necessary, to paraphrase Marx. Religion has inspired art much more naturally and easily, and with better results, than any kind of secular ideology, which may serve as another indication of their affinity. I will not deal here with the effect of religion on art as a source of inspiration, since this separate topic has been dealt with extensively in art history.

A survey of the scholarly literature on religion would reveal that the basic similarity between art and religion has been noted and expressed more than once. Specifically, there are two traditions which deal with this notion, one anthropological and the other psychoanalytic. The earlier psychoanalytic references are within the framework of psychoanalytic ego psychology, and the later ones within the framework of object relations theory. In anthropological and sociological literature both classical and contemporary expressions of this notion can be found. Malinowski, in his great work, *Magic, Science, and Religion* (1925)—which is really an important contribution to the psychology of religion—quotes rather approvingly Jane Harrison, who has said that

"Art and religion alike spring from unsatisfied desire" (cf. Harrison 1948). Raymond Firth is one scholar who has explicitly made the same claim I am making here regarding the basic nature of religion:

> Religion is really a form of human art, a symbolic product of human anxiety, desire, and imagination expressed in a social milieu. Like any art, religion is a product of tension—between the ideal and the actual, between the individual and the mass, between the urge to satisfaction and life, and recognition of the inevitability of suffering and death. A religion is distinguished from other arts by three main criteria. Its most effective expressions are generated, as in all arts, by individual creative effort, but they depend more than other arts upon tradition and membership in a community. Again, while every art has its forms and ceremonies to guard its practice, the rituals of religion tend to be so frequent, elaborate, evocative, and mandatory that they provide very strong guidelines for faith. Then, the rules of religious interpretation and conduct, unlike those of science and philosophy or the visual arts, are given a legitimacy of ultimate authority which is regarded as absolute and unchallengeable by those who subscribe to them. Now politics has been variously described as the art of the possible, or the art of the plausible. However this may be, one basic character of religion is clear—after a certain point it becomes the art of the implausible, in the sense of resting upon postulates which are nonempirical, which claim an inner rather than an outer appearance of truth, since they may run counter to what are ordinarily thought of as natural laws. In this promise to provide explanations which go beyond the world of sensory experience lies much of the appeal of religion. (Firth 1981, 584)

In the literature of psychoanalysis, the Freudian notion of illusion is used to explain both art and religion in a way strikingly similar to Jane Harrison's, as the fulfillment of unsatisfied or unattainable wishes through imaginary means. Kardiner (1939, 1945), combining psychoanalysis and anthropology, defines both art and religion as cultural projective systems. The mechanism of projection is basic to a psychological understanding of art, and it is basic in some theories of religion, notably Freud's and Marx's. According to psychoanalytic conceptions, religion is a projection of early family relations onto a cosmic screen. According to Marx, religion is an upside down projection of social relations in the real world. In both cases there is a creative process involved.

Ego psychology views the whole of human behavior as adjustment efforts on the part of the ego, and it assumes that the ego's defense mechanisms and defense maneuvers are the basis for both art and religion: art and religion are ways in which humans turn away from direct coping with reality. Kris (1952) and others have referred to a "regression in the service of the ego." There are obvious reality limits on how much humans can regress, and how often. That is why art may be regarded as a luxury that we cannot always afford. Continuing the line developed by Kris, Brenner (1966) spoke of this regression in the service of the ego as it appears ". . . in intellectual and artistic creativity, in the enjoyment of works of art, in religious activities . . ." (Brenner 1966, 395).

Winnicott (1971) offers a fascinating conceptualization of the basic processes common to art and religion, and he refers explicitly to both: "I am therefore studying the substance of *illusion* [italics in the original], that which is allowed to the infant, and which in adult life is inherent in art and religion, and yet becomes the hallmark of madness when an adult puts too powerful a claim on the credulity of others" (3). This "substance of illusion" is also the basis for "play, . . . artistic creativity and appreciation, . . . religious feelings, dreaming, fetishism, lying and stealing, . . . and the talisman of obsessional rituals" (5). Winnicott arrived at this conception through the study of transitional objects such as the infant's first possession, the proverbial "security blanket" to which it is extremely attached. The relationship to this object is the model for a special mode of experiencing. According to Winnicott:

> Transitional objects and transitional phenomena belong to the realm of illusion which is at the basis of initiation of experience. This early stage in development is made possible by the mother's special capacity for making adaptation to the needs for her infant, thus allowing the infant the illusion that what the infant creates really exists.
> The intermediate area of experience, unchallenged in respect of its belonging to inner or external (shared) reality, constitutes the greater part of the infant's experience, and throughout life is retained in the intense experiencing that belongs to the arts and to religion. (14)

A close reading of Winnicott brings us a surprising finding. His idea of the "intermediate area of experience" really parallels the ego-psychological notion of "regression in the service of the ego." Winnicott's explanation follows:

> It is assumed here that the task of reality-acceptance is never completed, that no human being is free from the strain of relating inner and outer reality, and that relief from this strain is provided by an intermediate area

of experience which is not challenged (arts, religion, etc.). This intermediate area is in direct continuity with the play area of the small child who is "lost" in play. (13)

This "relief from strain" is exactly what Kris (1952) and others discuss as the reason for the regression in the service of the ego. And this "relief from strain" may indeed be the drive behind both art and religion.

The important theoretical contribution by Pruyser (1976) draws attention to various similarities between religion and art, following mainly the psychoanalytic tradition. The psychological response to art and religion is based on similar processes. Both art and religion exist as social institutions for the same reasons: to provide gratification through fantasy. Art in practice, for both the artist and the audience, involves the combination of imagination and emotional arousal. So does religion. In religion, as in art, we have the involvement of producers (artists), products of the artists' work, and an audience who is responding to the artist through the product. Religion, like art, according to Pruyser, is the product of being made possible by uniquely human qualities. The psychological process of responding to religion is similar to the process of responding to other forms of art. It includes the activation of the human capacity for imagination and fantasy, and the involvement of such processes as identification, projection, displacement, and reaction-formation.

Religion as Art: Basic Elements

The three elements in the production of art—creator, product, and audience—are involved in both the private process of aesthetic experience and the more social processes of the production and the consumption of art. Truzzi (1978) notes that in addition to the three sets of categories involved in art as a social process, there are additional human actors who are vital for its existence:

In addition, each of these three central categories has associated roles for *mediators* or facilitators. These consist of the many institutionalized roles and social groupings that may be found attendant to each of the three more basic sets. Thus there are those involved in such things as the training of artists (e.g., director of an art school), the caretaking and cataloging of art products (e.g., museum curator, collector), the bringing of and communication about art products to its audience (e.g., dealer, theatrical producer, critic). These mediators may, in fact, often be more important to the condition of an art form than its producers, the products, or the audience.

Thus, in our society, distribution of a work is the key to success. A movie must be seen, a symphony must be heard, and marketing and publicity may be more important than any aesthetic considerations. (282)

Similar facilitators can be found in the institution of religion as well, and they are most active in its continuing functioning.

There are two major social roles in art: the role of the creator and the role of the audience (spectator, consumer). Kreitler and Kreitler (1972) suggest that concentrating on the role of the creator in art leads to the study of artistic motivation, creativity, uniqueness of artistic creativity, and the development of artistic creativity. Concentrating on the role of the audience in art leads to the study of the psychological processes involved in experiencing art, the development of the experience of art, and the effects of the experiences of art. Exact parallels for these concepts can serve in developing psychology of religion.

Great religious leaders and mystics may be seen as equivalent to great artists: theologians and philosophers of religion may be compared to art historians and art critics, and the great mass of believers to art audiences and consumers. Studies can concentrate on religious creators, i.e., religious innovators, leaders and saints, or they can examine the religious audience of common believers in their common experience of religion as a social reality. Spectators, in both art and religion, far outnumber creators; truly creative individuals in either field are few and far between. Kris and Kurz (1979) have collected a great number of stereotyped anecdotes and legends, so often connected with the names of artists. These materials reveal a clear biographical formula, which aims to describe the artist as a culture hero, endowed with special powers, who survives trials and tribulations to end up as a triumphant magician. This formula is almost identical to that dealing with religious heroes and saints. The artist is a secular saint, but in earlier times he was not completely secular, and divine powers were often attributed to him.

The psychology of art assumes a certain unity of basic processes, which are involved in all forms of art. Now I suggest that the same processes are involved in religion. The process of artistic creation is a model for understanding the process of religious creation. Individual (and group) reactions to religion can best be interpreted by looking at individual and group reactions to art. Both art and religion are based on human imagination and emotional involvement (or emotional "arousal"). These are the necessary conditions for the existence of both. There are, of course, cognitive, conscious processes involved in the creation of art that are as crucial as the presumed unconscious ones.

There is an individualistic bias in the psychology of religion, and a similar individualistic bias appears in the psychology of art. The individual does not invent his own religion and does not come to experience it individually. Art, likewise, is neither created nor experienced outside of social relations. A social system creates both religion and art. For the past one hundred years there has been in the literature a common emphasis on the personal and private nature of the religious experience. And what is more private, personal and ineffable than the aesthetic experience, which is much more common than the ecstatic "religious experience" described by James (1902)? Actually, I am following here a respectable classical tradition in the psychology of religion. The classical theory, which started the tradition of the American psychology of religion, emphasized private personal experiences as the cornerstone of the study of religion (Beit-Hallahmi 1974). The theory attempted here seeks to analyze further the nature of that private experience.

In religious ritual the artistic elements are most obvious and most conscious. The ritual is designed as a drama that enacts the relationship between the believer and the deity. Ritual is a highly structured repetition of a religious drama, designed to heighten emotions and commitments. The aesthetic nature of the experience is conscious and intentional: much conscious effort is put into making ritual as artistically successful as possible. Even a sermon is first of all an artistic product, which has to capture attention and keep it, shed a new light on a common experience, and arouse strong feelings. When I participate in a religious ritual, or when I have a religious experience, I am an actor. The difference between ritual and individual experience is in the stage on which the drama is played out. Ritual provides ready-made structure. In individual experience I am both actor and playwright. Séguy (1977) has discussed the production and the control of emotion by various conscious and deliberate means, which he has termed *éléments de spectacle*, in religious ritual. He implies an awareness of the artistic process of ritual on the part of religious institutions. The goal of artistic technologies is to enable us, the audience, to put a distance between ourselves and our normal reality testing. That is why art needs special expressive styles, and the same expressive styles exist in religious rituals. Literary style (as opposed to everyday language) takes us away from reality. Poetry is less reality related than prose, and special religious language has similar effects. The kind of coping that is represented by the two human activities of art and religion is characterized by being expressive, magical, or imaginary, and that special kind of coping, different from instrumental coping, is based on several basic psychological mechanisms.

Religion as Art: Identification and Catharsis

Inspiration and identification are two terms crucial to the understanding of both art and religion. The mechanism of identification, which is so essential to art, operates selectively, according to given cultural constraints. Through the mechanism of identification every member of the audience can participate in the unfolding drama on stage: in the case of religion, he can participate in a drama set on a cosmic stage. Any religious myth is a fantasy, created to serve the needs of both creator and audience. To be acceptable to the audience, it has to be reliable from a psychological point of view, not from any other viewpoint. This is the artistic, psychological truth of mythology.

Taylor (1981) describes the experience of a member of the artistic audience as follows:

> Certainly there is involvement, and an entering into. There is a transportation by means of, a sense of transcendence, a sense of being convinced by. The experience is compelling. One's attention is captured. One forgets oneself, even though the work may seem to integrate one into it, and the sense of this having happened is something integral to the whole experience. What is dropped, or forgotten, are the concerns or preoccupations with which one comes to the experience; or, if the experience organises them, what is dropped is the way they weigh with one. Skimming something off the detailed accounts to follow, we may say: in reading fiction we feel something is being made real for us; the poem brings something to life for us, it evokes its subject; the theatrical experience gives us a sense of having been transported into another reality (a reality other than the theatre in which we sit); the painting is something which absorbs and transforms us through its representational qualities; a piece of music seems to organise the environment in accordance with its own structure, and its own structure is something we interpret in what I will call for now "representational" (if rather indefinite) awareness. (3)

There have been attempts to define religion or "religious experience" through a special form of emotional arousal that is supposedly
involved in it. Defining religion by emotional arousal, "emotionality,"
or "catharsis" is a functional definition that is too broad to be useful.
Emotional arousal, emotionality, or catharsis can be found in various
human activities, most of which cannot be defined as religious. When
the process of emotional arousal in religion is examined closely, it
appears virtually indistinguishable from the process of emotional
arousal in situations which would be defined as secular. Ecstasy is to
be found among the participants in religious ceremonies, but it would
also be found among participants in rock concerts, football games, and
political rallies. The triggering of ecstasy by similar means, leading to
very similar results, can be seen in three varieties of American popular
culture: the revival meeting, the pop concert, and the college football
game. In all three rituals the effects of a mass setting, music, and
group identification, lead to a heightening of emotions, and to ecstasy
and exhilaration, warmth, joy, happiness—as the audience shares in
this state of emotional arousal. .

All religions offer opportunities for joy and sadness. Religious
rituals give the participants opportunities for ritual joy and for ritual
mourning. Believers rejoice at victories, salvations, and promises of
salvation; they mourn at the defeats of the just and faithful, of ancient
destructions and massacres. The ritual experiencing of victories and
defeats is capable of creating real catharsis, but there is an enormous
range of individual reactions to religious stimuli, ranging from no
response to sublime ecstasy. A whole range of private experiences is
common to both art and religion. Not every private aesthetic experience leads to ecstasy, nor does every private religious experience. Art
is a good starting point for understanding the gradations of individual
arousal in response to emotional stimuli. The gradations of emotional
arousal related to both art and religion may be adumbrated through
the following scale (from high to low): mystical experience, ecstasy,
catharsis, relief of tension, anxiety reduction, a pleasant feeling. All of
these terms describe levels of excitement and pleasure, and all represent experiences that occur in response to both religious and artistic
stimuli.

In both religion and art, ecstatic experiences are rare. The notion of
using "religious experience" as the starting point for the understanding of religion tends to obliterate this obvious fact. For most religious
people religion is experienced through routine rituals, rather than

through ecstasy. For most people art is experienced as mildly pleasurable, rather than ecstatically cathartic. For most religious believers, religious activities and involvements are remarkably nondramatic. There are no miracles, no religious crises, and no mystical experiences in their own lives.

Religion as Art: Illusion and Belief

From the nonbelieving observer's point of view, the question which creates the need for a psychology of religion goes as follows: "How can people believe in something which is so clearly an illusion?" One answer, which leads to the task at hand, is, "but in art they do it all the time, and nobody asks why." The suspension of disbelief is a precondition for the enjoyment of art and the acceptance of religion. (The enjoyment of religion as a form of art is not limited to believers. Even nonbelievers, such as I, enjoy religious stories, symbols, and rituals as a source of aesthetic pleasure.)

The basis for this experience is described by Taylor (1981) as follows:

> The fact that we have the ability to conceive of the "as if" is a central feature of human consciousness. Imagining, and being able to think of what is not the case, are clear instances of how fundamental this ability is to human thought. We can make it as though things are impinging upon consciousness when they are not, and this ability is one we put to use in a variety of ways. One of the possibilities for us, in this respect, is the creation of "as if" worlds that there is the possibility of us entering for their own sake. We can create situations and objects that are not the same as other situations and objects but which are like them. Moreover, we can see and respond to the likenesses we create although knowing that they are only likenesses. (177)

Unlike any other kind of art, a unique claim is made, in the case of religion, for the truth of the artistic message. The products of imagination are differentiated from the products of the secular artistic imagination by their special psychological status of holiness; they are proclaimed to be true, while art is always recognized as illusion. Thus, religion can be defined as that form of art which is claimed to be not just beautiful, but also true. What may be unique in the artistic process through which religion is created is that the creators of religion ascribe their artistic achievements to divine sources.

The question of truth is central to both religion and art, though in different ways. Adherents of a religion believe in the literal truth of its claims. Art audiences are likely to speak of "artistic truth," which is quite different. Following Freud (1927) I suggest that whatever truth there is in religion and art must be psychological truth.

One of the tasks of modern social science since its beginnings in the nineteenth century has been to explain the persistence and attraction of religion. The question of the persistence of religion in a rational world should be posed against the question of the persistence of art in the same. The question "how does religion survive in this modern, rational world?" immediately suggests a parallel question: "how does art survive in this modern, rational world?" The second question gives the answer to the first one. On the level of psychological theory, psychoanalytic ego psychology has suggested that there is a natural limit to rational reality testing, and the tension of rationality is relieved by opportunities for regression in the service of the ego, which creates both art and religion. There is, however, a more radical answer to these questions, given by Worsley (1968); it stems from the Marxist tradition of societal critique, and I find it convincing. In his analysis of Cargo Cults in Melanesia, Worsley states that the seeming irrationality of Cargo Cults is no less rational than the real irrationality of the capitalist social system. In Worsley's own words, "The type of social action taken by millenarists, then, does not represent an affectual regression from rational action, but a questioning of the validity of this very 'rationality'" (272).

Children tell imaginary stories, hear imaginary stories, and act out roles and events. They talk to unseen objects, create symbols, and are taught to share in cultural symbols. This early experience prepares the child for participation in the cultural institutions of art and religion. Religion is first learned through stories, not abstract principles (Pruyser 1976). The child is exposed to narratives, and is told that these imaginary stories have special significance in regard to himself and in regard to the whole culture, or even the whole world.

The normal course of acquiring religious beliefs, i.e., the way in which children acquire religious beliefs inside the family, is by learning simple stories and rituals. Only later is there any cognitive involvement in beliefs and arguments in favor of certain beliefs. Religion is a collection of moving stories and moving rituals. The stories are wonderful because they can move us so deeply and touch us so deeply. Mythology presents us with moving dramatic stories, into which we can, and do, project ourselves. The power of these moving stories is in creating powerful identification, and that is the power of art in every case. Religion is most often transmitted and learned not as a belief system in abstract principles, but as a system of narratives (myths, stories). Religious belief is first and foremost belief in certain narratives, which are experienced as true and significant. Beliefs are most often expressed as fantasies.

Belief is a certainty that *something happened*, that a certain story is true. Religion does not exist in the abstract, as a general acceptance of supernaturalism. For most concrete human beings in most concrete human situations (with the exception of some philosophers and theologians who are attempting to defend supernaturalism by making it abstract; see Kolakowski 1983), religion is a specific belief in a specific set of promises, claims, and stories. Psychology should aim at dealing with religion in the concrete reality of human history, the religion of real people rather than of the theologians (theologians are real; only their religion isn't). This means that the psychologist of religion deals with specific content, a specific text, if you will, that exists in the real world and calls for interpretation. Religion does not exist in the abstract. An individual is not just "religious." He is a Hindu, a Moslem, a Catholic, a Baptist.

I do not know a better expression of the reality of religious faith than William Blake's (1905) lines:

Scoffers

Mock on, mock on, Volaire Rousseau;
Mock on, mock on; 'tis all in vain!
You throw the sand against the wind,
And the wind blows it back again.

And every sand becomes a gem
Reflected in the beams divine;
Blown back they blind the mocking eye,
But still in Israel's path they shine.

The Atoms of Democritus
and Newton's Particles of Light
Are sands upon the Red Sea shore,
Where Israel's tents do shine and bright.

(P. 108)

This is the subject matter for the psychologist of religion, and all abstractions should grow out of it, not above it. William Blake's unshakable belief in specific, concrete, and vivid stories is the datum.

The question to be answered is that of the human capacity to imagine and believe, as it is expressed in concrete cultural forms. How and when do religious beliefs appear in the consciousness of the believer? Do they appear in the context of "ultimate concerns," or other concerns? Do they appear in connection with ideas about death, morality, or social divisions?

Religion as Art: The Audience

In the literature of the psychology of art, there is a common assumption of the basic similarities between creators and audiences in art, as far as basic psychological processes are concerned. As Berlyne (1960) stated, ". . . the creator, the performer, and the audience of a work of art . . . must, at least in some measure, be actuated by common motivational factors and reinforced by common sources of reward value" (229). According to the psychoanalytic view, both the creation and the enjoyment of art are based on identical psychological mechanisms, especially sublimation and regression in the service of the ego.

There has to be and there is a basic psychological readiness for art, as there is a basic psychological readiness for religion. The basic psychological processes involved are identical. The psychological processes involved in responding to religion on the part of the audience are similar to the process of responding to art. They include the activation of the imagination and the emotions, and an identification with elements of the artifact presented to the audience. The artistic product creates in the individual member of the audience reverberations, which go deep into his or her unconscious. Readers do not participate in the process the novelist went through in creating the novel, but it reverberates through their unconscious responses, and this approaches the original process of creation.

There is a gap, perhaps an unbridgeable one, between artist and audience. A similar gap exists between the creators of religion and the audience of religion. Since religious rituals, like classical art, have been preserved over long periods of time, the connection between original intentions (by the creators) and present experience is unclear. The artistic audience's distance from Shakespeare, El Greco or Bach is smaller than the religious audience's distance from credos, rituals, and prayers, sometimes dated more than a millennium, but preserved without changes. The problem of the distance between original intentions and current reactions in ritual and belief, and in art, is intriguing in several ways. One is the question of impact. Classical art, like classical religion, preserves its hold and impact on audiences a long time after its creation. The classics deal with eternal questions, in both religion and art. In the sphere of religion there is another gap between mediators and audiences, one which does not have to do with historicity. That is the gap between religion as given and religion as adopted. The official versions of religion, given by religious leaders and theologians, are always far removed from folk religion, the way in which people actually practice and (unofficially) create a living religious tradition. This gap can be compared to the parallel gap in art between high art and popular art. Routine religious activities can thus be compared not to high art but to entertainment, providing an easy, noncommittal outlet and emotional arousal. In theory, then, the number and characteristics of people in any society who are seriously involved in religion parallels the number and characteristics of people involved seriously in the arts. Both cases probably represent small minorities, with a possible overlap between the two groups.

In the response to art two parallel systems can be distinguished: one belongs to the experts, the other one to the common audience. In religion a similar gap between experts and audience can be described, with theologians and philosophers playing the role of art critics, passing judgments on the merits of religious creations. The difference between the art critics and the theologians is, of course, that the critics pass judgment on artistic merits only, and not on truth values. Art critics do not ever claim that a certain work of art has merits because it is veridical.

An interesting similarity between the social institutions of art and religion is in the nature of their audience. In modern Western societies (and possibly in other societies) the audience for both religion and art is largely made up of women, while the creators of both art and religion are men. Women are the customers for religion in all forms and for art in all its forms, more commonly than are men (Argyle and Beit-Hallahmi 1975). This may be because of women's lack of political and social power; they may have to cope through the creative use of imagination, since their ability to change reality is limited. In this respect women may resemble other oppressed groups.

These observations suggest one explanation for various findings in the social psychology of religion, such as the differences in religious involvement on the basis of sex, age, and family status: an inverse relationship seems to exist between readiness and opportunity for instrumental coping on the one hand, and involvement in religion and magic on the other hand.

Religion as Art: The Question of Consequences

Looking at art and related processes may lead to insights about one of the persistent questions in the contemporary psychology of religion: the question of effects or consequences. The question is often asked with a degree of amazement: "Why don't we find any behavioral effects of religious participation? Why doesn't going to church on Sunday have any effect on behavior during the rest of the week?" The effects of religious experience and rituals should be compared to the effect of artistic experiences, since the processes involved are so similar. This question will be asked with less amazement when the comparison to art is made.

The effects of religious rituals and beliefs can be compared to the effects of art. There is an obviously satisfying quality about art, psychologists would not expect any of this satisfaction to linger on and to affect one's behavior outside the specific situation of the art-ritual, be it a theater or a museum. They do not expect any consequences after finding out that a certain individual attends chamber music concerts every Wednesday. They might be able to say something about him in terms of social background and education, but they will rarely venture a guess as to his moral qualities or personality structure. Has anybody ever been ruined (or saved) by listening to Beethoven, reading Proust, or looking at a Van Gogh painting?

The major function of art has been considered, since the days of Aristotle, that of catharsis, i.e., the production of a (vicarious) emotional experience, through the arousal and ventilation of strong emotions. It is unclear whether such catharsis is likely to lead to other, instrumental behaviors. If one looks at religion through the catharsis perspective, he or she can then understand its limited behavioral consequences. If one adopts a Marxian perspective, it becomes clear that religion exists to serve this catharsis function, thus supporting the existing social arrangements by providing an expressive outlet to instrumental frustrations.

There are many human activities that are engaged in for themselves, without any additional consequences expected, and such activities are indeed referred to as "art" or "entertainment." If psychologists do not expect any effects in subsequent behavior when people go to museums, theaters, or athletic events, why should they expect any effects when people go to church? Do you expect any effects from a weekly visit to a museum or a concert, similar to the ones you expect from religion? Once this analogy is made, things become clearer. It is possible to have an emotional experience, a catharsis experience, or an ecstatic experience, without any lasting, or even short-term, effects. One can recall numerous occasions of artistic catharsis or ecstasy which were not followed by any lasting changes in behavior (despite the presumed "ennobling effects" of art). Actually, the value of artistic experiences may lie in their temporariness. Remaining in a state of catharsis or ecstasy for long is something most of us cannot afford, psychologically and socially.

The puzzle of the presumed effects of catharsis is clarified once it is realized that people search again and again for catharsis experiences, either in secular art or in religion. There is apparently no permanent or cumulative effect to catharsis. That is why the experience has to be repeated in various ways. People are ready to participate again and again in religious and artistic events that provide them with opportunities for emotional expression and ventilation. In other words, the effect of the experience is in the experience itself, when relief is provided. This relief, like all human satisfaction, is temporary, and has to be attained repeatedly.

There should be only minimal behavioral consequences to artistic experience, because it provides only an imaginary solution to behavioral problems. (Art relieves tensions and neutralizes them, and thus should have some behavioral consequences.) The imaginary relief of both art and religion should have some consequences, but their appreciation should be a matter of sensitive gauging. It may be that the behavioral consequences of art and religion are noticeable when there is an identity involvement or ego-involvement; this possibility will be examined in the second element in my presentation.

9

FIRST ATTEMPT AT A THEORY: RELIGION AS IDENTITY

Identity is one of the most popular words in contemporary social science parlance and even in the language of the mass media, but a close examination of its uses will reveal that it is often ill-defined, vague, and misunderstood. We are all supposed to be in the throes of an "identity crisis," but when psychologists examine the phenomena that most commonly receive that label, they realize that an identity crisis may mean several different things. The popularity of the term "identity" can only be compared to the popularity of the term "schizophrenia," which is just as badly abused and misunderstood in everyday usage (cf. Langbaum 1977).

I intend to examine, first, several theoretical uses of the term "identity", and then to will look at how this term is used in the research literature on religion. Then I will propose a possible way of using the concept in theorizing about religion as a cultural institution and as a human creation. The theoretical sources for the understanding of religion as a form of identity and as a way of attachment come from modern psychoanalytic theories and also from social psychology, sociology, and anthropology.

Traditions of Thinking about Identity

COLLECTIVE IDENTITY

The first goal and the basic necessity for every group is survival. This necessitates group integration and the creation of a common world view, at least in matters relevant to the group's existence and activities. Thus "the function of the group ethic, of course, is simply to maintain the group" (LaBarre 1972, 14). Collective identity of religious communities is deliberately and consciously fostered, in addition to its unconscious, spontaneous components. Social demarcations are introduced when the need to emphasize the "we," as different from or opposed to "they," is felt. As Zerubavel (1982) states: "There are many ways in which groups can and do stress their in-group unity as well as their distinctiveness vis-a-vis other groups. Language, emblems, dress, and dietary laws are just a few of the various characteristics almost universally employed by groups in order to distinguish group members from 'outsiders' (284)."

Collective identity is then expected to manifest itself in the individual's consciousness and behavior, in his "social self" (James 1890). James expressed first the idea of the reference group, when he stated that a person has "as many social selves . . . as there are distinct groups of persons about whose opinions he cares" (James 1890, 294). After James, it was Cooley who discussed the importance of group memberships for the individual (Cooley 1900). "Classical" sociologists, such as Park (1928), Stonequist (1937), and Hughes (1945), discussed stable membership as opposed to marginality, thus preceding Lewin (1948). Sherif (1948) formulated the classical distinction between "membership group" and "reference group," in addition to contributing to the conceptualization of ego-involvement in social psychology. Lewin's (1948) conception of group identity focuses on in-group solidarity, group boundaries, and intergroup relations. An individual's identity, as denoting group membership, is a background determinant of individual behavior in many settings.

THE SOCIAL-PSYCHOLOGICAL DEFINITION OF IDENTITY

The social-psychological and sociological style of defining identity is through viewing it as a system of group memberships (McCall and Simmons 1978). An individual belongs to various groups, and each group is represented in individual consciousness as an identity label. Berger (1963) stated that "identity is socially bestowed, socially sustained, and socially transformed" (98) and has described it in the following way:

> Every society contains a repertoire of identities that is part of the objective knowledge of its members. . . . As the individual is socialised, these identities are internalised. They are then not only taken for granted as constituents of an objective reality "out there" but as inevitable structures of an individual's own consciousness. The objective reality, as defined by society, is subjectively appropriated. In other words, socialisation brings

about symmetry between objective and subjective reality, objective and subjective identity. (1973; 275)

> Identity, with its appropriate attachments of psychological reality, is always identity with a specific, socially constructed world. . . . One identifies oneself, as one is identified by others, by being located in a common world. (1973; 277)

Parsons (1968) has defined identity as ". . . the pattern-maintenance code system of the individual personality" (20). Identity, according to this definition, maintains personal continuity through the coherent organization of information about the individual.

D. R. Miller (1963) presents the best articulation of social identity as a concept in social psychology. He limits the discussion to definitions, meanings, and evaluations arising in the course of social interactions, and describes identity as a structure, with a core-region called self-identity, a periphery called public identity, and an intermediate region of subidentities, which are tied to social roles. Miller's approach enables us to achieve an integration of the sociological tradition of identity as a label and the dynamic tradition of identity as a dynamic structure (ego-identity, according to Erikson). Identity and subidentity are useful social-psychological concepts which provide a bridge between individual personality and social tradition. Miller (1963) discusses the "public-objective" identity (identity as perceived by others), "public-subjective identity" (individual's perception of his public identity), and "self-identity" (the individual's perception of his social attachments). The structure and the content of identity are regarded as something that is determined by forces external to the individual and is not tied or related to personality dynamics.

A similar social-psychological definition of identity has been offered by Zavalloni (1975): "Demographic variables such as social class, sex, religion, ethnic and national origin, etc., may be seen as the objective components of social identity characterizing the Self as the perceiver, and its encoding of these elements will reflect his subjective identity" (200). Zavalloni then proceeds to list the following elements in a "social identity cluster": sex, nation, religious origin, political ideology, social class, family situation, age group, and profession. But, as Zavalloni (1972) suggests, just because a person states and knows his belonging to a group, what does that reveal about his commitment to it, or about its effects on his personality? What is the meaning, for the individual, of "belonging"? It may be positive, negative, or indifferent. A social category has to be assessed in relation to the ego, and that is where the classical social-psychological concept of ego-involvement (Sherif and Cantril 1947) comes in.

EGO-IDENTITY

Erikson's concept of ego-identity (1956, 1959, 1968) stems out of the psychoanalytic tradition and is related to the psychoanalytic concepts of identification and internalization (Bronfenbrenner 1961; Miller et al. 1968; Meissner 1970). The psychoanalytic tradition within which the concepts of identification and ego identity have been developed emphasizes, quite naturally, unconscious processes, which are hard to detect or quantify. In Erikson's (1956) formulations, the ego-identity is the stable (or unstable) center of the ego, and not a social label. It can belong only to an individual, not to a group. Erikson (1964) finds a relationship between the individual achievement of identity and the group identity: "True identity, however, depends on the support which the young individual receives from the collective sense of identity characterizing the social groups significant to him: his class, his nation, his culture." (93). "Ego identity, then, in its subjective aspect, is the awareness of the fact that there is a self-sameness and continuity to the ego's synthesizing methods, the style of one's individuality, and that this style coincides with the sameness and continuity of one's meaning for significant others in the immediate community" (Erikson 1968, 50).

But, as Zavalloni (1975), states, "Erikson . . . is extremely vague on the nature of this 'something' which links individual and group identity" (200). Ego-identity, for Erikson (1956, 1968) is an achievement, not a universal attribute of humanity. It is a final stage in personality development. One either achieves ego-identity or suffers from ego-identity diffusion. This is the way in which the concept of ego-identity has been understood in psychological literature (Beit-Hallahmi 1977b; Rasmussen 1964; Simmons 1970).

As Dashefsky (1974), suggested, "Ego-identity refers to the psychological core of what the individual means to himself (herself) (Erikson 1963, 261–262). Since it is conceived of as an unconscious phenomenon, it can best be dealt with on the empirical level through the clinical interviews of the psychiatrist or psychoanalyst" (241).

The ego-psychoanalytic conception of identity as the basis for sameness and continuity in behavior, following Erikson and Lichtenstein (1977), is best illustrated by Holland (1978, 1979), when he writes about ". . . sameness as a theme [in] . . . the recurring patterns in someone's life" (Holland 1979, 7), and uses individual examples of "identity themes" such as "Saul sought from the world balanced and defined exchanges, in which he would not be the one overpowered" (8). The flavor of internal, unconscious, personality dynamics is clearly evident.

Religious beliefs—or belonging to a religious group—may serve as an important source of support for an ego-identity system. This is clearly implied by Erikson's (1956) theory. Regarding the significance of religion to ego-identity, Argyle and Beit-Hallahmi (1975) state that "there is no clear evidence that religion helps with problems of individual identity and purpose. Nevertheless, it is significant that there is a peak of interest in religion, especially in its intellectual aspects, at or shortly before the age at which identity problems reach their height" (182).

THREE LEVELS OF IDENTITY

There have traditionally been two very different ways of conceptualizing identity. One is derived from the psychoanalytic literature, and the other from the literature of social psychology and sociology. The former relies on clinical data and centers around personality dynamics. The latter centers around group membership and its consequences. The former involves less precise conceptualizations and measurements. The latter enjoys better measurements and clearer findings.

While the concept of ego-identity (Erikson 1950) denotes the integration and stability of the individual personality, the concept of identity used in most of the social-psychological and sociological literature, following Lewin (1948), denotes membership in an externally-defined social group and the individual's integration into the group. Furthermore, on the social-psychological level it is quite clear that internal group cohesion is linked to intergroup divisions. It is the attachment to a particular group that is likely to lead to intergroup conflicts (Miller 1972). The literature of the last few dacades thus presents two distinct uses of the term "identity." The first is that of identity as a social group label and its psychological reflections. The second is that of an internal, dynamic structure.

I believe that the findings of both approaches—of clinical psychology and of social psychology and sociology—can be integrated through the adoption of a three-level conceptualization of identity. At the top I would place collective identity, i.e., identity as defined by the group, in its concern for distinctions (Habermas 1977). In the middle I would place social identity labels, as used by the individual and by others to identify him(self). At the bottom or deepest level I would place ego-identity, which is privately or even unconsciously experienced by the individual. Table 1 summarizes these three levels and proposes their relations to religion.

Dashefsky (1974) pointed to the many ambiguities in the usage of the terms "identity" and "identification" in social science literature, and he offered a framework for analysis of the meanings of identity for the individual. While Dashefsky's analysis is useful and important, he concentrates on the individual level. The question he leaves unresolved is the link between individual self-conceptions of social identity and collective religious identity.

Table 1: Summary of Identity Concepts and Their Uses

Concept	Source	Relation to Religion
Collective identity	Lewin (1948)	created by religious communities, consciously or unconsciously
Social identity, made up of several sub-identities	Miller (1963)	the religious subidentity may be one component among others, consciously reported
Ego-identity	Erikson (1956)	the religious subidentity may be a source of support and integration for the individual ego-identity

Religious Identity and Religion as Identity

The three conceptual levels of identity correspond to three empirical levels, of ego-identity, social identity, and collective identity. For most individuals, religion operates on the second level, as a social identity label. When I speak of religion as identity, I am speaking about religion at the group level, expressed by the individual and experienced by him as a label. This level may be regarded as rather superficial, but it covers much of what takes place in most societies under the heading of religion. Religious identity can be compared to other large or small group identities, to political identity, or the support for a certain political party. Religious identity and religious beliefs are the products of social learning; the whole research literature on religion attests to that.

Basic social identities, those of religious community, social class, and political group, if any, are learned within the boundaries of the family. Religion is most often learned and acquired within the family, as are all primordial roles. Only in a small minority of believers is there a choice of religious identity after a process of search and deliberation, outside one's family of origin. For most people there exists, in their experiencing of religion, what should be called the primacy of identity. First they find out, quite early in life, that they belong to a certain group. This first perception may be quite childish, but later this belonging becomes more tangible and concrete, and then beliefs are quite correctly perceived as tied to a certain group membership.

For most individuals, religion exists as part of their identity. They do not believe in a certain religious system; they are members of a religious group, Catholics, Jews, or Moslems. The only choice most individuals make, if they can make a choice at all regarding the dominant religious belief system in their group, is a sociometric one: whether they will follow group tradition.

Thus, most individuals don't choose a religion; they are simply born into one. And they learn their religion in the same way they learn other aspects of their social identity. After they have acquired an identity, they have to discover, sometimes to their utter surprise, that they have also acquired a system of beliefs that is tied to that identity. Thus, being Catholic means believing in certain things, while being Jewish means believing in other things. And since religion is part of social identity, most people simply follow the religion they have learned. A few people adopt a religion as a result of a conscious quest; for ninety-nine percent of religious people all over the world, religion is part of their conventional identity.

The distinction commonly adopted by sociologists and anthropologists can be applied here: in most cultures, for most human beings, religious identity is ascribed rather than achieved (Pi-Sunier and Salzmann 1978). That is, for most human beings religious identity—a distinctive religious group affiliation and respective beliefs—is not a matter of real learning or adoption, but a matter of social location. Indeed, Gordon (1969) has developed a categorization of answers to the Twenty Questions Test (Kuhn 1969) in which the first set is that of "ascribed" characteristics, which include designations conferred on the individual at birth: sex, racial and national heritage, and religious categorization.

The social psychology of religion and the sociology of religion deal with the identity level of religion, the level of the identity label and its consequences. The "religion of identity" concept is sufficient to explain much of the social-psychological findings on religious behavior. At this superficial level much of what is normally considered religious activity takes place.

The literature of research on religious behavior and its correlates shows quite readily that religious identity is most commonly used as identical with religious affiliation (e.g., Wimberley and Christenson, 1981). "Identity" is used synonymously with "affiliation," "orientation," "membership," and "denomination". The book by Argyle and Beit-Hallahmi (1975) is a repository of findings that relate to the effects of religious identity labels as reflecting differences among religious collectivities. There are indeed such differences, and thus the identity label can serve as a useful predictor. Religious identity labels are good predictors of socioeconomic indicators, such as educational level, urbanicity, occupational composition, and income (Goldstein 1969). Thus, we can safely predict that in the United States, on the whole, Jews will be better educated than both Catholics and Protestants, and that Protestants will be better educated than Catholics. Religious beliefs can be predicted from religious identity. In this way religious identity is unlike personality characteristics, which are not good predictors of many behaviors.

THE TWO PSYCHOLOGIES OF RELIGION: OF HIGH AND LOW EGO-
INVOLVEMENT

Through the three-tiered structure of identity concepts—from collective identity, via social identity, to ego-identity—the question of religious identity and its effects can be appropriately dealt with. The question for each individual is that of any possible contacts between the collective identity and his ego-identity. Is his religious identity just a matter of identity label, or does it have a role to play in the internal dynamics of his ego-identity? The most crucial question regarding religious identity is that of its centrality for the individual, in other words, ego-involvement. To what extent does the individual see his identity label as part of himself? For most individuals, religion exists, and makes a difference, only at the level of a social identity label, i.e., as it denotes group membership. Only for a small minority does religion have an impact on an emotional, high ego-involvement level, the level of art. At this higher level, individual experiences range from a moving experience at a ritual, to a personal "religious experience."

Two different psychological theories might be developed to explain two different kinds of religious involvement. One is the low-involvement religion, the religion of identity, learned within the family of origin and having little emotional significance; and the other is the high-involvement religion, often the religion of converts, who learned it outside their family of origin and invest much emotional energy in it. This distinction refers back to the concept of ego-involvement, which is a part of the classical heritage of social psychology. Sherif and Cantril (1947) described ego-involvement in the following words: ". . . the ego is a genetic formation made up of a host of personal and social values and . . . these values serve the individual as a frame of reference by means of which he makes those judgments that affect *him;* that define for *him* success and failure; that determine *his* loyalties and allegiances; that spell out what he conceives to be *his* role, *his* status, *his* class. Judgments and behavior resulting from this identification of oneself with a certain constellation of values we can properly term 'ego-involved'" (152–53). The term "ego-involvement" facilitates dealing with identity not as a label that the individual accepts passively or rejects, but with various levels of accepting one's identity and being committed to it. It thus becomes possible to speak of levels of ego-involvement, and of the religion of high ego-involvement and the religion of low ego-involvement. Most of the research previously devoted to the correlates of religious identity can safely be subsumed under the heading of the religion of low ego-involvement.

Psychologists can make predictions about low ego-involvement religiosity, and they can make useful predictions about high ego-involvement religiosity. The classical concept of ego-involvement can be used synonymously with the more modern concept of commitment, described by Maddi (1970) as the ability to believe in the truth, importance, and interest value of what one is doing and therefore the tendency to involve oneself fully in life situations and social institutions.

Religion gains its power on the individual level when it becomes tied to one's ego-identity, when it is imbued with high ego-involvement. The question is not one of stable or unstable ego-identity, but of high and low ego-involvement. Persons with both stable, or "successful", ego-identities and unstable ego-identities may have high and low levels of ego-involvement in regard to their religious identities. A threat or an insult to one's externally defined social identity is a threat or insult to one's self only if there is a sufficient degree of ego-involvement in that socially given label. The psychology of identity, as a social-psychological concept, should contribute to understanding the so-called "persistence of religion" (Allport 1950). Religion is preserved where social forces keep it as part of a group identity, and it is often promoted as such.

Every religious group aims at reaching a high level of ego-involvement among its members. This is done through socialization, and through the rituals of religious loyalty. The aim of every religious group, in socializing and resocializing its members and potential members, is to make sure that their religious identity becomes the object of high ego-involvement. Then they are going to become "true believers" (Hoffer 1951), ready to live and die for their faith. Indeed, in some cases religious groups require those who join them to change their formal identity by adopting a new name. This is clearly a way of fostering or forcing high ego-involvement through external identity symbols. A name change creates special expectations, not just in the person involved but in those around him, and it is likely to push him toward higher involvement and stronger identification with the group.

The truth claims of religion, and of all religions, carry with them a special emotional load because they are tied to personal identity, which means a high ego-involvement with group identity. Believing that one is a member of a small community of the elect, chosen by cosmic forces to put things on earth in order, does have a powerful impact on one's behavior. This is an identity label that is likely to lend support to one's ego-identity and also to lead to remarkable acts on both individual and group levels.

Conclusion: Religion as Identity

Religion is both personal and social, individual and cultural. The concept of identity seems to provide a bridge between the private and the public realms in religion, as an appropriate locus for that which connects the individual personality and the cultural matrix. An individual identity is made up of several subidentities, and the religious subidentity may be one of those.

Labels used to define religious affiliation structure one's identity in social space. This label is imposed from the outside, and it may not lead to real ego-involvement; however, much effort is put into making the identity label into social reality. While in most cases the identity label is no more than a passive acceptance of a social convention, the religious community will make it into a central identity structure. Social groups identity may be described as a loyalty structure, and as such it is reinforced and maintained by rituals of loyalty.

To use the term suggested by Mol (1978), religion sacralizes identity and thus contributes to social integration. This sacralization is maintained by four mechanisms, as described by Mol (1976): objectification, in which the social order is projected beyond the temporal commitment; emotional involvement; ritual, and myth. Religion becomes the basis for social identity by creating differences between groups, and it then becomes an ideology, a system of identity maintenance. The differences between religious groups in mythology, rituals, and customs all create social divisions, or at least serve to express existing social divisions.

The truth claims of religion are tied to identity. These beliefs are true not only because of their intrinsic merits, but also because they are a part of me. And beliefs may serve an important function in enhancing self esteem through social identity. Religion may compensate for objective suffering and inferiority by creating a group identity of the chosen, who are truly superior despite their worldly misery. The few may be chosen and superior because of their possession of the truth and their promised future salvation. There are endless examples of messianic groups who are secure in their expectation of imminent salvation despite the lack of any objective indications for that.

The uniqueness of religion as a system of beliefs and attitudes is often alleged to be its high degree of resistance to change, and its high degree of emotionality. Both can best be explained in terms of the identity system. Religion as a belief system is so persistent because it is tied to a personal sense of identity. Every challenge to a religious belief is a threat to the identity system, and people react strongly to such threats. The religious groups make sure, through the process of religious socialization, that religious beliefs are indeed tied to one's sense of identity, so that one will be ready to defend these beliefs if necessary. Identity then becomes the meeting ground for cognition and emotion, and these meetings have been known, of course, to lead also to battlegrounds. When religious beliefs are part of the self system, every challenge to the religious system becomes a challenge to the self. Individual differences in the closeness of the religious system to the core of the self may explain the differences in ego-involvement or religious commitment.

Whereas there is little "instrumental" value in religion, identity is instrumental in the sense of having behavioral consequences. It is easy to locate the behavioral consequences of religion as identity. Social identity has social consequences in behavior, and these consequences are not hard to discover. When we can correlate voting patterns with religious affiliation, we are clearly dealing with the consequences of identity in social life. Examples of the political implications of religious identity are not hard to find nowadays in most parts of the world, and much current suffering can be traced to various consequences of religious identity claims. In Israel today, for example, we can observe individuals who claim that their religious identity obliges them to oppress and dispossess other people (Beit-Hallahmi 1973a).

Religion in its identity function supports the existence of human community, but the existence of multiple human identities and multiple human communities may be dysfunctional in the long run, as it creates social divisions. Group identity, which exists to create social divisions, is a problem and an obstacle for religion, indeed, for all of humanity. Particularistic identities have created both political and religious counteridentities, which aim at one universal human self-hood. The dream of a universal human identity exists in religion and in politics. Universal religions seek to unify all of humanity, while universalistic ideas, such as Marxism, seek to unify humanity on secular basis. These dreams represent a natural yearning for overcoming human divisions, but the roots of group identity are deep and go back to early experiences in the human family. Every group identity starts with family identity.

Identity on the individual level is a necessary support system for the ego, as the ego cannot survive without both ego-identity and social group identity, and as the ego cannot survive without structures around it, and so both ego-identity and social group identity serve as vital support structures. The discussion of religion and identity leads to a possibly more basic psychological tendency and a more basic source of religious feelings, and that is the process of (and the need for) attachment to human objects. Here lies the most basic urge of all human urges, which gives its energy to most human activities and human institutions.

Religion is claimed to be true because it is essential for the maintenance of a certain identity, like other kinds of ideology. Thus religion is an identity-maintenance system, serving as the basis for social divisions and social grouping.

RELIGION AS ART AND IDENTITY

The term "art" has been used here to circumscribe the individual level of involvement in religion, whereas the term "identity" has been used to refer to the social level of involvement and its consequences. The discussion of religion as art follows the classical historical emphasis on individual religious experience, which has dominated the psychology of religion since William James. The discussion of religion as art follows the classical historical emphasis on individual religious experience, which has dominated the psychology of religion since William James. The discussion of religion as identity follows the tradition of the social psychology of religion. The art and identity model is able to explain on the one hand the lack of visible consequences of religion on an individual level, and on the other hand the clearly visible consequences of religion on a social level.

Religion offers us a case of unique connection between art and identity. Religion is a form of art that is claimed to be representing reality, rather than reality transformed by imagination, and that is utilized to define and actualize an identity. Viewing religion as representing social realities is a conception tied to the names of both Karl Marx and Emile Durkheim (both, incidentally, descended from distinguished rabbinical families). Durkheim has expressed this view most directly when stating that religion cannot be false, in a social sense, because it represents society and social relations. Against the psychological truth of religion, recognized by Freud, we may posit the social truth of religion, recognized by Durkheim. Carrying these two views one step further, within my framework here, I may say that Freud posits religion as art, while Durkheim posits it as social identity.

The psychoanalytic explanation for the function of both art and religion emphasizes gratification through fantasy. We go to church for the same reason that we go to the movies, because the fantasies presented at both places are gratifying. Going to church is in addition an expression of an identity, and identity may be just as important as fantasy for some individuals in determining religious behavior. One may venture in parallel between the intrinsic-extrinsic dichotomy, proposed by Allport and Ross (1967), and the art and identity factors. The intrinsically religious individual responds to religion as art. The extrinsically religious responds to religion as identity. This analysis is, of course, historical. It is possible that in other times and other places the psychological context of religion was different. Today, in the age of secularization, religion has to compete very hard for its audience against other, more popular forms of art and entertainment, and its effects as an identity system is also diminishing.

In order to go further in the usage of the two concepts, I would like to propose a typology: a religion of art and a religion of identity. Based on the well-known distinctions between religious activity in different social groups (Argyle and Beit-Hallahmi 1975), this typology incorporates the two kinds of involvement presented in table 2.

Table 2: Typology of Religious Actions

RELIGION OF ART	RELIGION OF IDENTITY
intense experience	social activity
intrinsic	extrinsic
sect	church

The discussion of religion and identity leads to a possibly more basic psychological tendency and a more basic source of religious feelings, and that is the process of, and the need for, attachment to human objects. Here lies the most basic urge of all human urges, which gives its energy to most human activities and human institutions. The basic psychological process of attachment operates in art, where there is attachment to imaginary objects, internalized and then externalized. It clearly operates in the case of social identity, where the underlying process is that of attachment to real objects.

This observation suggests a new psychological definition of religion: religion is a form of art, about which a claim is made that it represents reality, and which also expresses both individual and group identity. It is the identity element which is responsible for the fact that this particular form of art is claimed to be true. It is claimed to be true because, like other kinds of ideology, it is essential for the maintenance of a certain identity. Thus religion is both an art and an identity-maintenance mechanism serving as a basis for social divisions and social groupings.

CONVERSION AS A RESEARCH FOCUS

Historically, religious conversion has been the focus and the model for research and theorizing in the psychology of religion. Since the days of James and Starbuck, it has been the model and the center of research in all traditions and approaches. Understanding why is not too difficult. The dramatic change in religious identity, accompanied by intense religious experiences, is rare and unusual. Ninety-nine percent of religious believers have never considered changing their religious identity, which in ninety-nine percent of the cases was inherited from their parents. Those unusual individuals who take the effort to consider other options represent the religion of high ego-involvement. They deserve the curiosity and scrutiny of social scientists. It is through looking at conversion that they may discover basic processes having to do with religion as both art and identity. After one hundred years of work, conversion is still the area of much interesting work in the psychology of religion (see Hunsberger 1980; Paloutzian 1981; Ullman 1982). Dramatic identity change can be found in varied cultural contexts, as it reflects, on the individual level, the appearance of new religious movements (Beit-Hallahmi and Nevo 1987).

EPILOGUE: INTEGRATING THE STUDY OF RELIGION AND THE DISCIPLINE OF PSYCHOLOGY

The problem of the integration of the psychology of religion within psychology in general has to do with how both are conceived. Today it is quite clear that the psychology of religion is outside the mainstream of academic psychology (Beit-Hallahmi 1977a; Gorsuch 1988). A changed conception of the science of psychology will enable such an integration. The current lack of interest on the part of academic psychology in religion, both theoretically and practically (in terms of research), is not that different paradigmatically from the situation in regard to other significant social behaviors (How much attention does academic psychology give to art?). In the tough-minded academic psychology of today there is little room for the study of religion. Such a study requires a historical and humanistic approach, and cooperation with the traditional humanities and "softer" social sciences.

It may be claimed, with justification, that most research in the psychological study of religion is unsystematic. That is, it is rarely guided by a general model or paradigm. Often, it takes the form of a correlational study done on a sample of convenience, through the use of a questionnaire created especially for that particular study. In this way, a quantity of disparate findings is collected, without any real advance in systematic knowledge. However, the above description fits many areas of psychology, and not just the study of religion. Academic psychologists studying religion merely follow the accepted etiquette of research production.

The relationship between the psychological study of religion and academic psychology in general may be assessed by the extent to which general principles or psychological theories are applied to the study of religion. The truth of the matter is that, first, there are few accepted general principles in psychological theory, and, second, to the extent that such principles exist, they are not often applied to the study of religion. Research questions in the psychological study of religion are not usually formulated as a test of some general theory or principle; more often than not they are internal to the field. One ready example is the distinction between intrinsic and extrinsic religiosity referred to earlier. This concept came out of the need felt by some psychologists to explain the positive correlation between religiosity and ethnic prejudice. Allport and Ross (1967) suggested a dimension of religiosity which distinguished between the deeply devout and the conventionally religious. The explanation was that the latter contributed to the correlation, but not the former. In this case, no general psychological theory was used to explain the finding; instead, a concept specific to the psychology of religion was introduced. There has been an attempt, however, to explain this finding in general social-psychological terms. Ehrlich (1973) suggested that the positive correlation between prejudice and religiosity is explained by the primary factor of conventionality: conventional people are both religious and prejudiced, and hence the correlation. This explanation, however, was taken up by only a few people in the psychology of religion.

The cry may be heard that the reason much research on the psychology of religion is unsystematic is that the field lacks a major coherent theory. This claim is worth examining. What should a psychological theory of religion explain? What is a good theory in the psychology of religion? Ideally, a psychological theory of religion should be a general theory of human actions and consciousness, in which religion is but one instance of more general principles. Universal elements in religion and culture are the subject matter of the psychology of religion. The world of the spirits is universal, created by universal processes of the human psyche. It is projection of the internal psychical world of objects. In fact, a good theory in the psychology of religion does exist, and that theory is psychoanalysis.

Freud and James told us that though religion may be an illusion, its psychological sources are real and effective. Religious involvement stems from the deepest layers of man's consciousness and experiences. One thing psychologists need to remember is that emotion is the fuel which keeps many religious flames alive. It was Freud who enabled psychologists to relate the strength of religious emotions in the individual to the individual's development history. Depth psychology gives an answer to the question of the universal potential for religion: if there is indeed such a universal readiness, it must stem from the universal nature of those early universal conflicts which religion reflects and projects. If, as Freud suggested, religion reflects the yearning and fears tied to the early objects in the child's life, then the universal experience with these objects creates the readiness to echo religious sentiments.

What Freud emphasized, in contrast to various apologists for religion, was that the strength of human emotions involved in religious activities and experiences is no proof for the validity of religious beliefs. The source of these emotions, according to psychoanalysis, is internal; they are no indication of a response to something "out there," but an indication of needs and anxieties within the human psyche. Freud's insights may help in understanding the two faces of religion as a social force—the eros and thanatos of religion. It may be a force for love and brotherhood, when human beings are drawn together by a common belief and a common attachment. It may also be a force for hatred, ranging from the moral indignation of the preacher to the lethal fanaticism of the crusader, both guided and driven by the burning flames of a cruel superego, reflected and projected in the fires of hell.

One thing that has to be remembered in connection with Freud's historical hypothesis is that explanations for the historical origins of religious acts may not be identical or relevant to the motivation for such acts at present. That is, it is possible that a certain religious act is a sublimation and ritualization of some prehistorical event or custom, but the person following this religious custom today is not aware of this origin and may be doing it for completely different reasons.

Many academic psychologists are made uneasy by the psychoanalytic emphasis on the unconscious and the invisible. But when psychologists analyze fantasies, they have to base their analysis on a theory which regards human fantasy as its subject matter. It is quite clear that behaviorism does not have much to say about religion, beyond the fact that it serves a social control function. Reading Skinner (1953) on religion is one of the best arguments for a dynamic psychology of religion. The behavioristic analysis turns out to be merely a boring and narrow description, without any explanations whatsoever. Another conclusion can be reached—and another answer to the question of why religion is not studied more often by psychologists. If the best available theory for understanding religious phenomena, psychoanalysis, is almost banished from the groves of academic psychology, and if the whole approach of academic psychology to human actions is still acultural and ahistorical, then it is not surprising that religion is not a very appropriate topic for psychological research. The psychology of religion has to be historical and cultural, and it will flourish only within a psychology that is cultural and historical. While few would expect a rise in the popularity of the psychoanalytic paradigm within academic psychology, it will continue to be one of the dominant paradigms in the study of religion outside of psychology.

"Religious suffering is at the same time an expression of real suffering and a protest against real suffering. Religion is the sigh of the oppressed creature, the heart of a heartless world, and the soul of soulless conditions. It is the opium of the people" (Marx 1964, 43–44). If Freud provides us with the basis for a depth psychology of religion, this well-known and eloquent quotation can serve as the basis for a social psychology of religion in the contemporary world. Marxian ideas are especially enlightening if we want to understand the functions of religion in a secularized world. In the rationalized world of advanced industrial society, religion may be indeed the heart of the heartless world and the soul of soulless conditions. More effective kinds of opium now dominate the market, but religion still offers a shelter, a sanctuary from dehumanized reality, and a heaven from alienation. The needs satisfied by religion are real and intense, while its answers are illusory and harmful.

The intensity of responses to religious solutions may be one indication of real psychological deprivations. The enthusiastic adherents of old and new gurus try to heal the deep wounds left in their souls by our mechanized, cruel world. Theirs may be a false consciousness, but their pain is never false. Marx (Marx and Engels 1957; Marx 1964) offered his own theory of psychological projection as the source of religion. His view of religion in relation to the real world leads to several interesting predictions, both social and personal. If religion is indeed a projection of the mysteries and deprivations of the real world, then we can expect two things: first, more religiosity in oppressed groups, and second, more emotion in the religiosity of the oppressed. More specific predictions can be derived from Marxian ideas, as follows:

A. People who experience actual deprivations are more likely to be religious.
B. The holding of religious beliefs should be positively correlated with holding conservative social and political views and negatively correlated with the holding of radical political views.

C. Holding religious beliefs should be negatively correlated with objective knowledge of the social and political world.
D. Holding religious views should be negatively correlated with actions which aim at changing social conditions.
E. Holding religious views should be positively correlated with actions aimed as the preservation of the social order.

Research on the social psychology of religion has provided much support for these predictions (Photiadis and Schnabel 1977; Argyle and Beit-Hallahmi 1975).

Ideas for revising the philosophy of our specialized field should consider the calls for the renewal of psychology as a discipline. Gergen (1973) in summarizing his view of the state of social psychology, suggested that ". . . the study of history, both past and present, should be undertaken in the broadest possible framework. . . . A concentration on psychology alone provides a distorted understanding of our present condition" (319).

The movement to turn psychology into a humanistic field of inquiry will make it easier to find within it a home for the psychology of religion. Cronbach (1975), in proposing a new manifesto for psychology, states: "The goal of our work . . . is not to amass generalizations atop which a theoretical tower can someday be erected. . . . The special task of the social scientist in each generation is to pin down the contemporary facts. Beyond that, he shares with the humanistic scholar and the artist in the effort to gain insight into contemporary relationships, and to realign the culture's view of man with present realities. To know man as he is, is no mean aspiration" (126).

The definition of boundaries between the psychology of religion and other disciplines has been worked in practice. What happened in the field, so to speak, in the places where psychologists of religion carry out their work and present the fruits of their work (in conferences, libraries and scholarly journals), is that contributions to the field were not made only by psychologists. Sociologists and anthropologists have opened up the field and have made psychological contributions. Trying to keep from crossing disciplinary boundaries becomes futile since the issues do not define themselves according to the conventional boundaries, so that the answers cannot be limited by those boundaries. There are no purely psychological questions in the psychology of religion, so that there are no purely psychological answers.

Any attempt to understand religion as a human phenomenon has to be interdisciplinary, ". . . a combination of psychological and cultural points of view" (Wallace 1966, vii). Psychoanalysis, while being in conflict with the dominant paradigm in academic psychology, fits well with a historical, cultural, and humanistic emphasis. While psychoanalytic theory provides the grounding for an understanding of the world of spirits as a creation of the human psyche, the specific cultural projections onto the world of spirits have to be examined in relation to anthropology and history. Psychology of religion should become part of the study of cultures, or the science of culture, which would include the shared and collective experiences of humans in cultural groups. In such an enterprise the concept of identity should be central for the psychological viewpoint. Instead of the behavioral sciences— ahistorical and acultural—we should have the cultural sciences: psychology, anthropology, and sociology, collaborating with the traditional humanities. Psychology of culture should cover art, literature, religion, ritual, symbols, and cultural communication. Within such a psychology of culture there will be room for the development of a comprehensive psychological study of religion.

REFERENCES

Adorno, T. W., E. Frenkel-Brunswick, D. J. Levinson, and R. N. Sanford. 1950. *The authoritarian personality.* New York: Harper.

Alatas, S. H. 1977. Problems of defining religion. *International Social Science Journal* 29:213–34.

Allport, G. W. 1950. *The individual and his religion.* New York: Macmillan.

———. 1978. *Waiting for the lord: thirty-three meditations on God and man.* New York: Macmillan.

Allport, G. W. and B. M. Kramer. 1946. Some roots of prejudice. *Journal of Psychology* 22:9–39.

Allport, G. W., and J. M. Ross. 1967. Personal religious orientation and prejudice. *Journal of Personality and Social Psychology* 5:432–43.

Anderson, C. H. 1968a. The intellectual subsociety hypothesis: An empirical test. *Sociological Quarterly* 8:210–27.

———. 1968b. Religious communality among academics. *Journal for the Scientific Study of Religion* 7:87–96.

Argyle, M., and B. Beit-Hallahmi. *The social psychology of religion.* London: Routledge & Kegan Paul.

Atkinson, J. W. 1974. Motivational determinants of intellective performance and cumulative achievement. In *Motivation and achievement,* ed. J. W. Atkinson and J. O. Raynor. Washington, D.C.: Winston.

Bakan, D. 1965. *Sigmund Freud and the Jewish Mystical Tradition.* New York: Schocken.

Batson, C. D. 1977. Experimentation in the psychology of religion: An impossible dream. *Journal for the Scientific Study of Religion* 16:413–18.

Beit-Hallahmi, B. 1973a. Religion and nationalism in the Arab-Israeli conflict. *Il Politico* 38:232–43.

———. 1973b. *Research in religious behavior: Selected readings.* Belmont, Calif.: Brooks/Cole.

———. 1974a. Psychology of religion, 1880–1930: The rise and fall of a psychological movement. *Journal of the History of the Behavioral Sciences* 10:84–90.

———. 1974b. Salvation and its vicissitudes: Clinical psychology and political values. *American Psychologist* 29:124–29.

———. 1976. On the "religious" functions of the helping professions. *Archiv für Religionspsychologie* 12:48–52.

———. 1977a. Curiosity, doubt and devotion. The beliefs of psychologists and the psychology of religion. *Current Perspectives in the psychology of religion,* ed. H. N. Malony. Grand Rapids: Eerdmans Publishing Company.

———. 1977b. Identity integration, self-image crisis, and "superego victory" in postadolescent university students. *Adolescence* 45:57–64.

———. 1978. *Psychoanalysis and religion: A bibliography.* Norwood, Pa.: Norwood Editions.

———. 1984. Psychology and religion. In *Psychology and Its Allied Disciplines,* ed. M. H. Bornstein. Hillsdale, N.J.: Lawrence Erlbaum Associates.

Beit-Hallahmi, B., and B. Nevo. 1987. "Born-again" Jews in Israel: The dynamics of an identity change. *International Journal of Psychology* 22:75–81.

Bellah, R. H. 1965. Father and son in Christianity and Confucianism. *The Psychoanalytic Review* 52:236–58.

Bellah, R. N. 1970. Response to comments on "Christianity and symbolic realism." *Journal for the Scientific Study of Religion* 9:112–15.

Bem, D. J. 1970. *Beliefs, attitudes, and human affairs.* Belmont, Calif.: Brooks/Cole.

Bereiter, C., and M. B. Freedman. 1962. Fields of study and the people in them. In *The American College,* ed. N. Sanford. New York: Wiley.

Berger, P. L. 1963. *Invitation to sociology.* Garden City, N.Y.: Doubleday.

Berger, P. 1973. Identity as a problem in the sociology of knowledge. In *Towards the Sociology of Knowledge,* ed. G. W. Remmling. London: Routledge & Kegan Paul.

Berlyne, D. E. 1960. *Conflict, Arousal and Curiousity.* New York: McGraw-Hill.

Betts, G. 1929. *The beliefs of seven-hundred ministers.* New York: Abingdon.

Black, M. 1962. *Models and Metaphors: Studies in Language and Philosophy.* Ithaca: Cornell University Press

Blake, W. 1905. *Poems of William Blake.* London: Routledge.

Bordin, E. S. 1966. Curiosity, compassion and doubt: The dilemma of the psychologist. *American Psychologist* 21:116–21.

Bordin, E. S., B. Nachmann, and S. J. Segal. 1963. An articulated framework for vocational development. *Journal of Counseling Psychology* 10:107–18.

Bouma, G. D. 1970. Assessing the impact of religion: A critical review. *Sociological Analysis* 31:172–79.

Bowser, A. 1977. Delimiting religion in the constitution: A classification problem. *Valparaiso University Law Review* 11:163–226.

Braginsky, B. M., and D. D. Braginsky. 1974. *Mainstream psychology—A critique.* New York: Holt, Rinehart & Winston.

Brenner, C. 1966. The mechanism of repression. In *Psychoanalysis—A General Psychology,* eds. R. M. Lowenstein, L. M. Newman, M. Schur, and A. J. Solnit. New York: International Universities Press.

Bronfenbrenner, U. 1960. Freudian theories of identification and derivatives. *Child Development* 31:15–40.

Brown, L. B. 1973. *Psychology and religion.* Baltimore: Penguin.

Burtchaell, J. T. 1970. A response to "Christianity and symbolic realism." *Journal for the Scientific Study of Religion* 9:97–99.

Campbell, D. F., and D. W. Magill. 1968. Religious involvement and intellectuality among university students. *Sociological analysis* 29:79–93.

Cattell, R. B. 1938. *Psychology and the religious quest.* London: Thomas Nelson and Sons.

Cavenar, J. C., Jr., and J. G. Spaulding. 1977. Depressive disorders and religious conversions. *Journal of Nervous and Mental Disease* 165:209–12.

Clark, E. T. 1929. *The psychology of religious awakening.* New York: Macmillan.

Clark, W. H. 1978. A follower of William James. In *Psychology and faith: The christian experience of eighteen psychologists*, ed. H. N. Malony. Washington, D.C.: University Press of America.

Coe, G. A. 1916. *The psychology of religion*. Chicago: University of Chicago Press.

Conklin, E. S. 1929. *The psychology of religious adjustment*. New York: Macmillan.

Cooley, C. H. 1900. *Human nature and the social order*. New York: Scribner's.

Cronbach, A. 1933. The psychology of religion. *Psychological Bulletin* 30:377–84.

Cronbach, L. J. 1975. Beyond the two disciplines of scientific psychology. *American Psychologist* 30:116–27.

Dashefsky, A. 1974. And the search goes on: The meaning of religio-ethnic identity and identification. *Sociological Analysis* 33:239–45.

Deconchy, J. P. 1967. *Structure genetique de l'idée de Dieu*. Brussels: Lumen Vitae.

———. 1977. Regulation et signification dans un cas de "compromis" ideologique (ecclasiastiques catholiques et propositions "marxistes"). *Bulletin de Psychologie* 30:436–50.

———. 1985. Non-experimental and experimental methods in the psychology of religion. In *Advances in the psychology of religion*, ed. L. B. Brown. Oxford: Pergamon Press.

Dittes, J. E. 1967. *The Church in the Way*. New York: Scribner's.

———. 1969. Psychology of religion. In *The handbook of social psychology*, ed. G. Lindzey and E. Aronson. Reading, Mass.: Addison-Wesley.

———. 1978. Christian style in academics and administration. In *Psychology and Faith: The Christian Experience of Eighteen Psychologists*, ed. H. N. Malony. Washington, D.C.: University Press of America.

Douglas, W. 1963. Religion. In *Taboo Topics*, ed. N. L. Farberow. New York: Atherton Press.

Durkheim, E. 1915. *The elementary forms of religious life*. London: Allen and Unwin.

Ehrlich, H. J. 1973. *The Social psychology of prejudice*. New York: Wiley.

Ellis, A. 1960. *Reason and emotion in psychotherapy*. New York: Lyle Stewart.

Erikson, E. H. 1950. *Childhood and society*. New York: Norton.

———. 1956. The problem of ego identity. *Journal of the American Psychoanalytic Association* 4:56–118.

———. 1958. *Young man Luther*. New York: Norton.

———. 1959. Identity and the life cycle. *Psychological Issues* 1:1–171.

———. 1963. *Youth and Challenge*. New York: Basic.

———. 1964. *Insight and responsibility*. New York: Norton.

———. 1966. Ontogeny of ritualization. In *Psychoanalysis—A general psychology*, ed. R. M. Loewenstein, et. al. New York: International Universities Press.

———. 1968. *Identity, youth and crisis*. New York: Norton.

———. 1969. *Gandhi's truth*. New York: Norton.

Faulkner, J. E., and G. DeJong. 1972. Religion and intellectuals. *Review of Religious Research* 14:15–24.

Festinger, L., H. W. Riecken, and S. Schachter. 1956. *When prophecy fails*. Minneapolis: University of Minnesota Press.

Firth, R. 1981. Spiritual aroma: Religion and politics. *American Anthropologist* 83:582–601.

Fishbein, M., and I. Ajzen. 1974. Attitudes towards objects as predicators of single and multiple behavioral criteria. *Psychological Bulletin* 81:59–74.

Frazer, J. G. 1951. *The golden bough.* New York: Macmillan.

Freud, S. [1927] 1961. *The future of an illusion.* New York: Norton.

————. [1907] 1959. Obsessive actions and religious practices. In *The standard edition of the complete psychological works of Sigmund Freud.* Vol. 9. London: The Hogarth Press.

Fromm, E. 1950. *Psychoanalysis and Religion.* New Haven: Yale University Press.

Gallagher, C. E. 1966. In testimony before the House Special Subcommittee on Invasion of Privacy of the Committee on Government Operations. *American Psychologist* 21:404–22.

Gergen, K. 1973. Social psychology as history. *Journal of Personality and Social Psychology* 26:309–20.

Glock, C. Y. 1962. On the study of religious commitment. *Religious Education* 57:S98–S109.

Glock, C. Y., and R. Stark. 1965. *Religion and society in tension.* Chicago: Rand McNally.

Goldstein, S. 1969. Socioeconomic differentials among religious groups in the United States. *American Journal of Sociology* 74:612–31.

Gordon, C. 1969. Self-conception. In *The self in social interaction,* ed. C. Gordon and K. Gergen, 114–36.

Gorsuch, R. L. 1978. Research psychology: An indirect ministry to the ministers. In *Psychology and faith: The Christian experience of eighteen psychologists,* ed. H. N. Malony. Washington, D.C.: University Press of America.

————. 1988. Psychology of religion. *Annual Review of Psychology* 39:201–21.

Gorsuch, R. L. and D. Aleshire. 1974. Christian faith and ethnic prejudice: A review and interpretation of research. *Journal for the Scientific Study of Religion* 13:281–307.

Guntrip, H. 1956. *Psychotherapy and religion.* New York: Harper & Row.

————. 1967. Religion in relation to personal integration. *British Journal of Medical Psychology* 62:423–33.

————. 1968. *Schizoid phenonema, object relations and the self.* New York: International Universities Press.

Gurin, G., J. Veroff, and S. Feld. 1960. *Americans view their mental health.* New York: Basic Books.

Habermas, J. 1977. On social identity. *Telos* no. 19:91–104.

Hall, G. S. 1904. *Adolescence: Its psychology and its relations to physiology, anthropology, sociology, sex, crime, religion, and education.* 2 vols. New York: Appleton.

Harrison, J. 1948. *Themis.* London: Cambridge University Press.

Hassenger, R., ed. 1967. *The shape of Catholic higher education.* Chicago: University of Chicago Press.

Henry, E. R. 1938. A survey of courses in psychology offered by undergraduate colleges of liberal arts. *Psychological Bulletin* 35:430–35.

Henry, W. E., J. H. Sims, and S. L. Spray. 1971. *The fifth profession.* San Francisco: Jossey-Bass.

Hoffer, E. 1951. *The true believer.* New York: Harper & Row.

Holland, N. N. 1978. What can a concept of identity add to psycholinguistics? In *Psychiatry and the humanities*, ed. J. H. Smith, 3:171–234. New Haven: Yale University Press.

———. 1979. Reading and identity. *Academy Forum* (American Academy of Psychoanalysis). 23:7–9.

Homans, P., ed. 1968a. *The dialogue between theology and psychology.* Chicago: University of Chicago Press.

———. 1968b. Introduction. In *The dialogue between theology and psychology*, ed. P. Homans. Chicago: University of Chicago Press.

———. 1970. *Theology after Freud.* Indianapolis: Bobbs-Merrill.

———. 1982. A personal struggle with religion: Significant fact in the lives and work of the first psychologists. *Journal of Religion* 62:128–44.

Hudson, L. 1972. *The cult of the fact.* London: Cape.

Hunsberger, B. 1980. A reexamination of the antecedents of apostasy. *Review of Religious Research* 21:158–70.

Hughes, E. C. 1945. Dilemmas and the contradictions of status. *American Journal of Sociology* 50:353–59.

Inkeles, A., and D. H. Smith. 1974. *Becoming modern.* Cambridge: Harvard University Press.

James, W. 1890. *Principles of psychology.* Vol. 1. New York: Henry Holland & Co.

———. [1897] 1956. *The will to believe.* New York: Dover Publications.

———. 1899. Preface. *The psychology of religion*, by E. D. Starbuck. New York: Scribner's.

———. [1902] 1961. *The varieties of religious experience.* New York: Collier.

———. 1907. *Pragmatism: A new name for some old ways of thinking.* New York and London: Longmans, Green.

Johnson, P. E. 1959. *Psychology of religion.* New York: Abingdon.

Jones, E. 1951. *Essays in applied psychoanalysis.* London: Hogarth Press.

———. 1953–57. *The life and work of Sigmund Freud.* London: Hogarth Press.

Kantor, J. R. 1969. *The scientific evolution of psychology.* Chicago: The Principia Press.

Kardiner, A. 1939. *The Individual and His Society.* New York: Columbia University Press.

Kardiner, A. and R. Linton. 1945. *The psychological frontiers of society.* New York: Columbia University Press.

Klein, D. E. 1981. *Jewish Origins of the Psychoanalytic Movement.* New York: Praeger.

Knapp, R. H., and J. J. Greenbaum. 1953. *The younger American scholar.* Chicago: University of Chicago Press.

Kolakowski, L. 1982. *Religion.* New York and Oxford: Oxford University Press.

Kreitler, H., and S. Krietler. 1972. *Psychology of the Arts.* Chapel Hill, N.C.: University of North Carolina Press.

Kris, E. 1952. *Psychoanalytic Explorations in Art.* New York: International Universities Press.

Kris, E. and O. Kurz. 1979. *Legend, Myth and Magic in the Image of the Artist.* New Haven: Yale University Press.

Kuhn, M. H. 1969. Self attitudes by age, sex and professional training. In *Social psychology through symbolic interaction*, ed. G. I. Stone and H. Farberman. Waltham, Mass.: Blaisdell.

La Barre, W. 1972. *The ghost dance.* New York: Dell.

Langbaum, R. 1977. *The mysteries of identity: A theme in modern literature.* New York: Oxford University Press.

Langer, S. K. 1953. *Feeling and Form: A Theory of Art.* New York: Scribner.

Lazarsfeld, P., and W. Thielens, Jr. 1958. *The academic mind.* Glencoe: Free Press.

Lee, R. S. 1948. *Freud and Christianity.* London: Clark & Co.

Lehman, E. G., and D. W. Shriver. 1968. Academic discipline as predictive of faculty religiosity. *Social Forces* 47:171–82.

Lehman, H. C., and P. A. Witty. 1931. Scientific eminence and church membership. *Scientific Monthly* 33:544–49.

Leuba, J. H. 1896. A study in the psychology of religious phenomena. *American Journal of Psychology* 7:309–85.

———. 1901. The contents of religious experience. *The Monist.* 9:4.

———. 1912. *A psychological study of religion.* New York: Macmillan.

———. 1916. *The belief in God and immortality.* Boston: Sherman, French and Company.

———. 1917. Ecstatic intoxication in religion. *American Journal of Psychology* 28:578–84.

———. 1926a. Psychology of religion. *Psychological Bulletin* 23.

———. 1926b. *The psychology of religious mysticism.* New York: Harcourt.

———. 1926c. Note on meetings and conferences for the discussion of the psychology of religion. *Psychological Bulletin* 23:729.

———. 1934. *Religious beliefs of American scientists. Harper's* 169:297.

Lewin, K. 1948. *Resolving social conflicts.* New York: Harper.

Lichtenstein, H. 1977. *The dilemma of human identity.* New York: Jason Aronson.

MacDonell, A. J., and D. F. Campbell. 1971. Performance and change in the religious dimensions of an intellectual elite. *Social Compass* 18:609–19.

Maddi, S. R. 1970. The search for meaning. In *Nebraska Symposium on Motivation*, ed. M. Page. Vol. 18. Lincoln: University of Nebraska Press.

Malinowski, B. (1925). Magic, Science and Religion. In *Science, Religion, and Reality*, ed. J. Needham. London: Macmillan.

Malony, H. N. 1972. The psychologist-Christian. *Journal of the American Scientific Affiliation* 24:135-44.

———, ed. 1978. *Psychology and faith: The Christian experience of eighteen psychologists.* Washington, D.C.: University Press of America.

Marcia, J. 1967. Ego identity status: Relationship to change in self esteem, general maladjustment, and authoritarianism. *Journal of Personality* 35:119–33.

Markle, G. E., J. C. Petersen, and M. O. Wagenfeld. 1978. Notes from the cancer underground: Participation in the Laetrile movement. *Social Science and Medicine* 12:31–57.

Marx, K. 1964. *Early writings.* New York: McGraw-Hill.

Marx, K., and F. Engels. 1957. *K. Marx and F. Engels on religion.* Moscow: Foreign Languages Publishing House.

Maslow, A. 1964. *Religions, values and peak experiences.* Columbus: Ohio State University Press.

McCall, G. J., and G. J. Simmons. 1978. *Identities and interactions.* Rev. ed. New York: Free Press.

McClelland, D. C. 1964. *The roots of consciousness.* New York: Van Nostrand.

Mead, G. H. [1934] 1964. Mind, self and society. In *G. H. Mead on social psychology. Selected Papers*, ed. A. Straus. Chicago: University of Chicago Press.

Meadow, M. J. and R. D. Kahoe. 1984. *Psychology of religion.* New York: Harper & Row.

Meissner, W. W. 1970. Notes on identification. 1. Origins in Freud. *The Psychoanalytic Quarterly* 39:563–89.

Merton, T. 1948. *The seven storey mountain.* New York: Harcourt, Brace.

Miller, A. A., G. H. Pollock, H. E. Bernstein, and F. P. Robbins. 1968. An approach to the concept of identification. *Bulletin of the Menniger Clinic* 32:239–52.

Miller, D. R. 1963. The study of social relationships: Situation, identity, and social interaction. In *Psychology: A study of a science.* 5th ed., ed. S. Koch. New York: McGraw-Hill.

Miller, J. 1981. Interpretations of Freud's Jewishness, 1924–1974. *Journal of the History of the Behavioral Sciences* 17:357–74.

Miller, L. 1972. Identity and violence. *Israel annals of psychiatry and related disciplines* 10:71–77.

Mol, H. J. 1976. *Identity and the Sacred.* Oxford: Blackwell.

———. 1978. Introduction. *Identity and Religion*, ed. H. J. Moll. London: Sage.

Mowrer, O. H. 1961. *The crisis in psychiatry and religion.* Princeton: Van Nostrand.

Muensterberger, W. 1972. The sources of belief. Introduction to G. Roheim, *The Panics of the gods*, New York: Harper & Row.

Oates, W. A. 1973. *The psychology of religion.* Waco, Tex.: Word Publishers.

Osarchuk, M., and S. J. Tate. 1973. Effect of induced fear of death on belief in afterlife. *Journal of Personality and Social Psychology* 23:256–60.

Page, F. H. 1951. The psychology of religion after fifty years. *Canadian Journal of Psychology* 5:60–67.

Paloutzian, R. F. 1981. Purpose in life and value changes following conversion. *Journal of Personality and Social Psychology* 41:1153–60.

———. 1983. *Invitation to the psychology of religion.* Glenview, Ill.: Scott, Foresman & Co.

Park, R. E. 1928. Human migration and the marginal man. *American Journal of Sociology* 33:881–93.

Parsons, T. 1951. *The social system.* New York: Free Press.

———. 1960. *Structure and process in modern society.* Chicago: Free Press.

———. 1968. The position of identity in a general theory of action. In *The self in social interaction*, ed. C. Gordon and K. J. Gergen. Vol. 1. New York: Wiley.

Pattillo, M. M., and D. M. MacKenzie. 1966. *Church-sponsored higher education in the United States.* Washington, D.C.: American Council on Higher Education.

Pepper, S. C. 1942. *World Hypotheses.* Berkeley: University of California Press.

Photiadis, J. D., and J. F. Schnabel. 1977. Religion: A persistent institution in a changing Appalachia. *Review of Religious Research* 19:32–42.

Pi-Sunier, O., and Z. Salzmann. 1978. *Humanity and culture*. Boston: Houghton Mifflin.

Pratt, J. B. 1907. *The psychology of religious belief.* New York: Macmillan.

———. 1908. Psychology of religion. *Harvard Theological Review* 1:435–54.

———. 1920. *The religious consciousness*. New York: Macmillan.

Pruyser, P. W. 1973. Sigmund Freud and his legacy: Psychoanalytic psychology of religion. In *Beyond the classics: Essays in the scientific study of religion*, ed. C. Y. Glock and P. E. Hammond. New York: Harper & Row.

———. 1976. Lessons from art theory for the psychology of religion. *Journal for the Scientific Study of Religion* 15:1–14.

Ragan, C., H. M. Malony, and B. Beit-Hallahmi. 1980. Psychologists and religion— professional factors and personal beliefs. *Reviews of Religious Research 21*, 208–17.

Rank, O. 1914. *The myth of the birth of the hero*. New York: Journal of Nervous and Mental Disease Publishing Company.

Rasmussen, J. E. 1964. Relationship of ego identity to psychological effectiveness. *Psychological Reports* 15:815–25.

Reck, A. J. 1967. *Introduction to William James*. Bloomington: Indiana University Press.

Reik, T. 1946. *Ritual: Psychoanalytic Studies*. New York: Farrar.

———. 1951. *Dogma and compulsion*. New York: International Universities Press.

Rizzuto, A. M. 1979. *The birth of the living God*. Chicago: University of Chicago Press.

Roe, A. 1952. *The making of a scientist*. New York: Dodd, Mead.

———. 1956. *The psychology of occupations*. New York: Wiley.

Rogers, D. P. 1965. Some religious beliefs of scientists and the effect of the scientific method. *Review of Religious Research* 7:70–77.

Rokeach, M. 1968. *Beliefs, attitudes, and values*. San Francisco: Jossey-Bass.

Rubenstein, R. L. 1963. A note on the research log in psychoanalytic studies in religion. *Jewish Social Studies* 25:133–44.

Schaub, E. L. 1922. The present status of the psychology of religion. *Journal of Religion* 2:362–65.

———. 1924. The psychology of religion in America during the past quarter century. *Journal of Religion*. 4:113–34.

———. 1926a. Psychology of religion. *Psychological Bulletin* 23:681–700.

———. 1926b. The psychology of religion in America. *Symposium* 1:292–314.

Séguy, J. 1977. Rationnel et emotionnel dans la pratique liturgique Catholique: Un modele theorique. *La Maison Dieu* 129:73–92.

Sherif, M. 1948. *An outline of social psychology*. New York: Harper.

Sherif, M., and H. Cantril. 1947. *The psychology of ego-involvement*. New York: Wiley.

Simmons, D. D. 1970. Development of an objective measure of identity achievement status. *Journal of Projective Techniques and Personality Assessment* 34:241–44.

Skinner, B. F. 1953. *Science and human behavior*. New York: Macmillan.

Spanos, N. P. and E. C. Hewitt. 1979. Glossolalia: A test of the "trance" and psychopathology hypotheses. *Journal of Abnormal Psychology* 88:427–34.

Spero, M. 1980. *Judaism and Psychology*. New York: Ktav.

Starbuck, E. D. 1899. *Psychology of religion*. New York: Scribner's.

Stark, R. 1963. On the incompatibility of religion and science; a survey of American graduate students. *Journal for the Scientific Study of Religion* 3:3–21.

Stark, R., et. al. 1971. *Wayward shepherds: prejudice and the Protestant clergy.* New York: Harper & Row.

Steinberg, S. 1973. The changing religious composition of American higher education. In *Religion in sociological perspective,* ed. C. Y. Glock. Belmont, Calif.: Wadsworth.

Stonequist, E. 1937. *The marginal man.* New York: Scribner's.

Strunk, O. 1957. *The present status of the psychology of religion. The Journal of Bible and Religion* 25:287–92.

Strunk, O., Jr. 1978. All things hold together. In *Psychology and faith: The Christian experience of eighteen psychologists,* ed. H. N. Malony. Washington, D.C.: University Press of America.

Szasz, T. S., and R. A. Nemiroff. 1963. A questionnaire study of psychoanalytic practices and opinions. *Journal of Nervous and Mental Disease* 137:209–21.

Taylor, R. 1981. *Beyond Art.* Sussex: The Harvester Press.

Thurstone, L. L., and E. J. Chave. 1929. *The measurement of attitude.* Chicago: University of Chicago Press.

Trent, J. W. 1967. *Catholics in college: Religious commitment and the intellectual life.* Chicago: University of Chicago Press.

Truzzi, M. 1978. Toward a general theory of the folk, popular, and elite arts. *Research in The Sociology of Knowledge, Science and Art* 1:279–89.

Tylor, E. B. 1871. *Primitive culture.* London: Murray.

Ullman, C. 1982. Cognitive and emotional antecedents of religious conversion. *Journal of Personality and Social Psychology* 43:183–92.

Wallace, A. F. C. 1966. *Religion: An anthropological view.* New York: Random House.

Watson, J. B. 1924. *Behaviorism.* Chicago: University of Chicago Press.

Wilson, B. R. 1966. *Religion in secular society.* London: Watts.

Winnicott, D. W. 1971. *Playing and Reality.* London: Tavistock.

Wimberley, R. C. and J. A. Christenson. 1981. Civil religion and other religious identities. *Sociological Analysis* 42:91–100.

Worsley, P. 1968. *The Trumpet Shall Sound.* New York: Schocken.

Wundt, W. [1912] 1916. *Elements of folk psychology.* Translated by E. L. Schaub. New York: Macmillan.

Zavalloni, M. 1972. Social identity: Perspectives and prospects. *Social Science Information* 12:65–91.

———. 1975. Social identity and the recording of reality: Its relevance for cross-cultural psychology. *International Journal of Psychology* 10:197–217.

Zerubavel, E. 1982. Easter and Passover: On calendars and group identity. *American Sociological Review* 42:284–89.

Zilboorg, G. 1967. *Psychoanalysis and Religion.* London: Allen & Unwin.

Zilboorg, M. S. 1967. Introduction to G. Zilboorg, *Psychoanalysis and Religion.* London: Allen & Unwin.

INDEX